Collins
PRIMARY
WORLD ATLAS

Globes and maps

Globes are models of the earth. The seven global views below show the true shape and size of the continents.

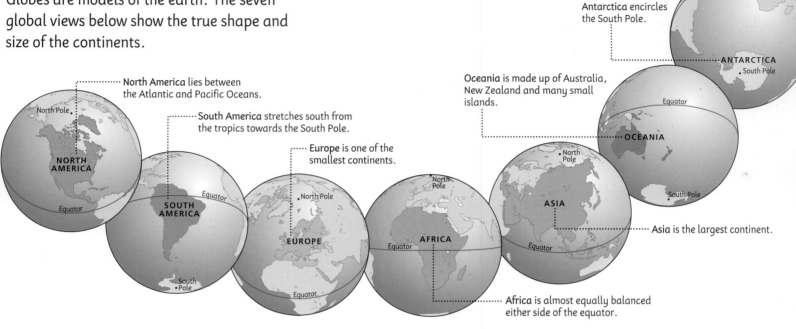

North America lies between the Atlantic and Pacific Oceans.

South America stretches south from the tropics towards the South Pole.

Europe is one of the smallest continents.

Antarctica encircles the South Pole.

Oceania is made up of Australia, New Zealand and many small islands.

Asia is the largest continent.

Africa is almost equally balanced either side of the equator.

Mapping the world

To show the world on a flat map we need to peel the surface of the globe and flatten it out. There are many different methods of altering the shape of the earth so that it can be mapped on an atlas page. These methods are called **projections**.

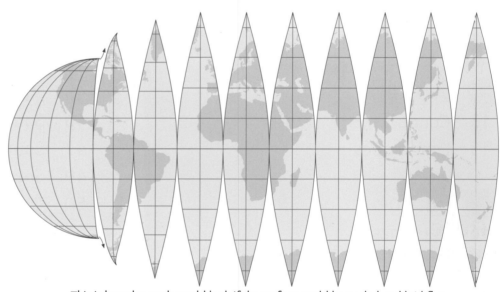

This is how the earth would look if the surface could be peeled and laid flat.

Projections

Map projections change the shape and size of the continents and oceans. The projection used for world maps in this atlas is called Eckert IV.

How the world map looks, depends on which continents are at the centre of the map. Compare the shape of Africa on the maps below to that on the globe.

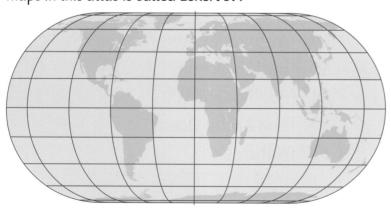

For UK atlases the world would look like this.

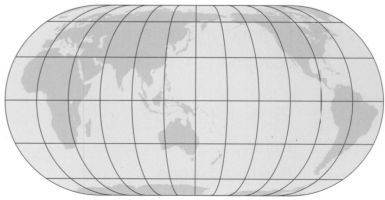

For Australian atlases the world would look like this.

Latitude and longitude

Every feature in the world can be located accurately. We use latitude and longitude to locate where features are. Latitude and longitude form our global positioning system.

Lines of latitude are imaginary lines which circle the earth. They are numbered in degrees North or South of the equator. Lines of longitude are imaginary lines which run from the North to the South Poles. They are numbered in degrees East or West of a line through London known as the Prime Meridian. We use the degrees to say where any feature is located.

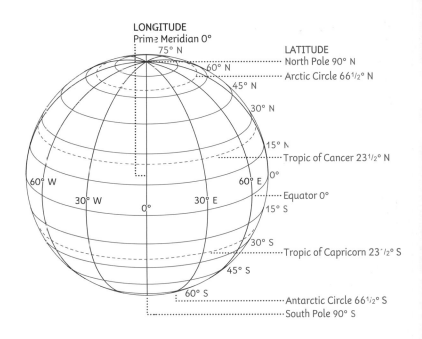

Grid references

Lines of latitude and longitude are used in this atlas to make a grid. By labelling the columns in the grid with a letter and the rows with a number a simple grid code e.g. B6 can be used to find all places within one grid square. This system is used in this atlas.

Cartagena is in B8

Bogotá is in B7

Piura is in A6

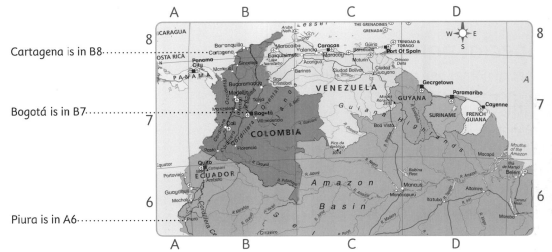

Hemispheres

The equator divides the globe into two imaginary halves. All land north of the equator is called the northern hemisphere. Land south of the equator is called the southern hemisphere. 0° and 180° lines of longitude also divide the globes into two imaginary halves, the western and eastern hemispheres.

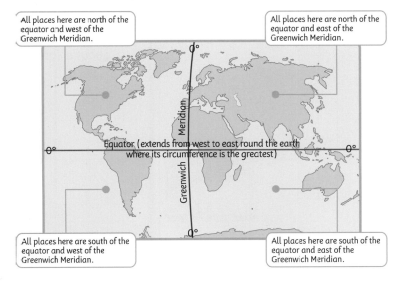

All places here are north of the equator and west of the Greenwich Meridian.

All places here are north of the equator and east of the Greenwich Meridian.

All places here are south of the equator and west of the Greenwich Meridian.

All places here are south of the equator and east of the Greenwich Meridian.

Equator (extends from west to east round the earth where its circumference is the greatest)

Direction

On most atlas maps you will find a compass. It names the four compass points North (N), East (E), South (S) and West (W). Between each main point are intermediate points Northeast, Southeast, Southwest and Northwest. These help us give more accurate directions.

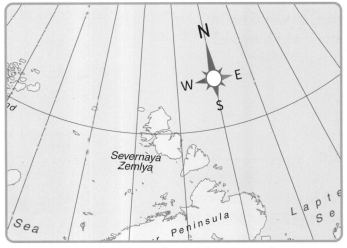

On atlas maps the north point always follows a line of longitude

Atlas maps

Atlas maps tell us about the various parts of the world. They tell us about different environments in the world.

Some maps show country shapes and where towns are located within the country. These are called political maps.

Some maps show landscapes. They show the physical environment.

Special names and numbers

Special names and numbers are used to label parts of an atlas map.

Title
This names the map area and describes what the map shows.

Page number
This helps you to find out where the map you want is in the atlas.

Locator map
This shows the part of the world covered by the map.

Area comparison
This map shows the size of the British Isles compared to the region mapped.

Scale
This explains how large a map is. It helps to work out distances between places. See page 6 to find out more about scale.

Compass
This always points north-south on the map. It shows east and west. Other directions can be found from the compass.

Key
This explains what the colours and symbols used on the map represent.

Fact boxes
These contain interesting information about a continent.

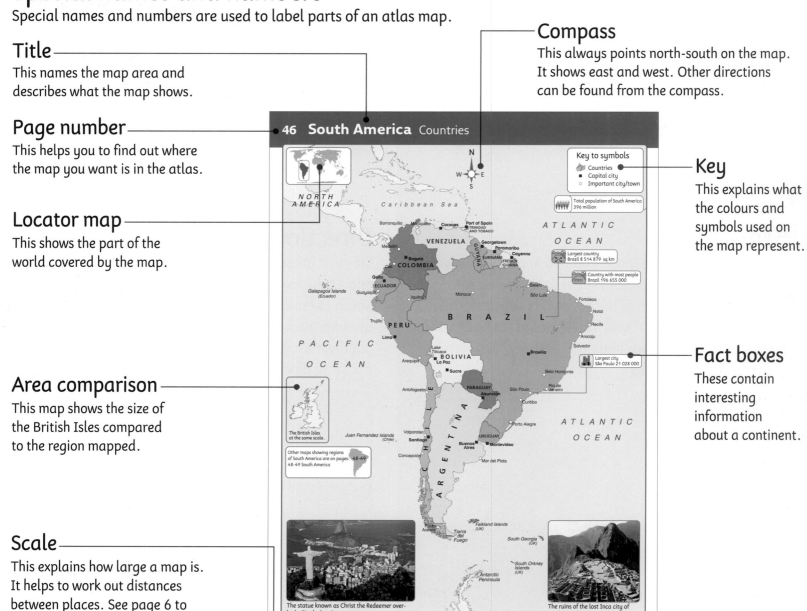

Map symbols

Maps are made up of symbols and names. The symbols can be points, lines or area colours.
A map is complete when the symbols and the names are combined.

Point symbols

■○ Town stamps
▲ Mountain peaks
⊘ Airports

Lines

—— Roads
┅┅ Railways
—— Rivers
—— Coastline

Area colours

▢ Lake/sea
◈ Country colours

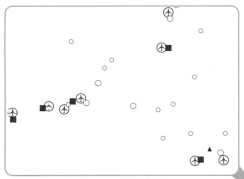

Point symbols are used on a map to show towns, mountain peaks and airports.

Lines are used an a map to show communications and drainage.

Area colours are used to distinguish one country from another and the land from the sea.

Names on atlas maps

The style and size of the type used on maps helps to explain what the name means.

Large bodies of water

PACIFIC OCEAN
Gulf of Guinea

Islands

Cuba
Bioco

Countries

N I G E R I A
BENIN

Large cities

Porto-Novo
Lomé

Small towns

Parakou
Enugu

Rivers

R. *Mississippi*
R. *Nile*
R. *Amazon*

Mountain peaks

Mount Cameroon
Everest

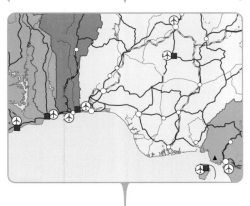

All the symbols are combined to show features and their correct locations.

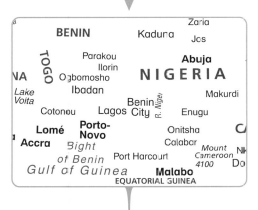

Names are needed to show places and features shown on the map. Only some places and features are named.

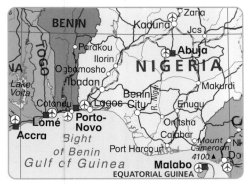

The map is complete when the symbols and the names are combined.

Scale

Maps are much smaller than the regions they show. To compare the real area with the mapped area you have to use a scale. Each map in this atlas shows its scale. This is shown using a scale bar which is explained in words.

E.g.

| 0 | 200 | 400 | 600 | 800 km |

Scale : One centimetre on this map is the same as 200 kilometres on the ground.

Large scale maps show smaller areas with more detail.

LARGE SCALE

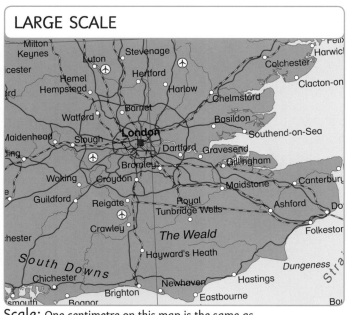

Scale: One centimetre on this map is the same as 20 kilometres on the ground.

| 0 | 20 | 40 | 60 | 80 | 100 km |

MEDIUM SCALE

Scale: One centimetre on this map is the same as 250 kilometres on the ground.

| 0 | 250 | 500 | 750 | 1000 | 1250 km |

Measuring distance

The scale of a map can be used to measure how far it is between two places. For example, the straight line distance between Boa Vista and Cayenne on the map to the right is 5 centimetres.

Look at the ruler.
One centimetre on this map is the same as 200 kilometres on the ground. The real distance between Boa Vista and Cayenne is therefore 1000 kilometres (i.e. 5 X 200).

| 0 | 200 | 400 | 600 | 800 km |

Scale : One centimetre on this map

Extend your knowledge and understanding by visiting these websites which provide lots of information and material to help with your homework and projects.

British Isles
Places to visit
Visit Britain www.visitbritain.com
Tourism in Ireland www.tourismireland.com
www.discoverireland.ie
Weather and climate
The Met Office www.metoffice.gov.uk
BBC weather www.bbc.co.uk/weather
Landscapes and rivers
Learning through landscapes www.ltl.org.uk
Learning rivers content.swgfl.org.uk/rivers
Scottish landscapes
www.bbc.co.uk/scotland/education/sysm/landscapes
Statistics
National statistics www.statistics.gov.uk/hub/index.html

Europe
European Union europa.eu/index_en.htm

World
Climate
World climate statistics www.worldclimate.com
Population
City populations www.citypopulation.de
Geography
Royal Geographical Society www.rgs.org/HomePage.htm
National Geographic www.nationalgeographic.com
Mountains
Mountains of the world www.peakware.com
Satellite images
Earth Observatory earthobservatory.nasa.gov
Visible Earth visibleearth.nasa.gov
MODIS satellite images modis.gsfc.nasa.gov
Development issues
Global Eye www.globaleye.org.uk
Flags
Flags of the world www.theodora.com/flags
International organisations
ActionAid International www.actionaid.org
The Commonwealth www.youngcommonwealth.org
Christian Aid
www.christianaid.org.uk/resources/games/index.aspx
United Nations www.cyberschoolbus.un.org

Small scale maps show larger areas with less detail.

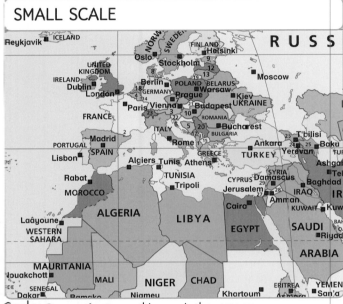

SMALL SCALE

Scale: One centimetre on this map is the same as 800 kilometres on the ground.

0   800   1600   2400   3200 km

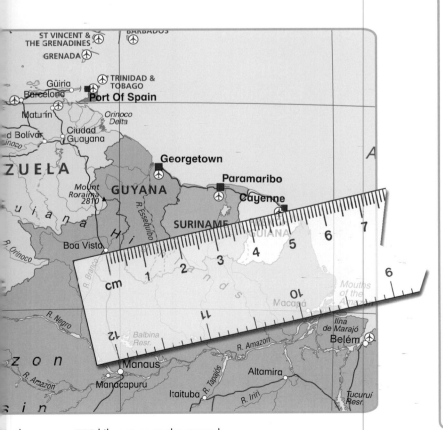

is the same as 200 kilometres on the ground.

The Solar System

The Solar System is the Sun and the many objects that orbit it. These objects include eight planets, at least five dwarf planets and countless asteroids, meteoroids and comets. Orbiting some of the planets and dwarf planets are over 160 moons. The Sun keeps its surrounding objects in its orbit by its pull of gravity which has an influence for many millions of kilometres.

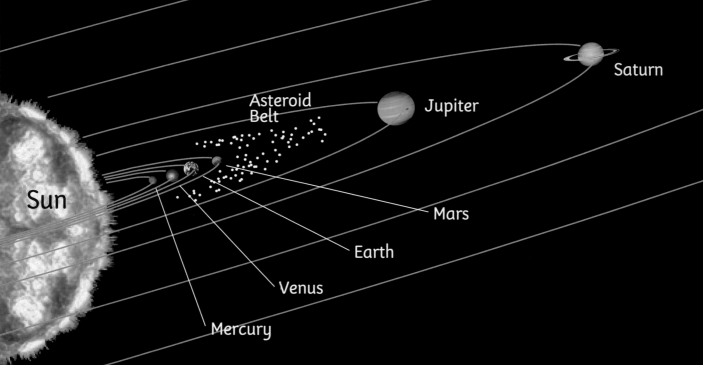

Saturn

Asteroid Belt

Jupiter

Sun

Mars

Earth

Venus

Mercury

Planets of the Inner Solar System

PLANET DISTANCE FROM THE SUN	Mercury 58 million kilometres	Venus 108 million kilometres	Earth 150 million kilometres	Mars 228 million kilometres
	Mercury is the smallest planet and closest to the Sun.	Venus lies between Earth and the Sun. It is the brightest object in the sky.	Earth is the only planet in the Universe known to support life. Most of its surface is covered in water.	Mars is known as the red planet. It has a mountain which rises 24 kilometres above the land.

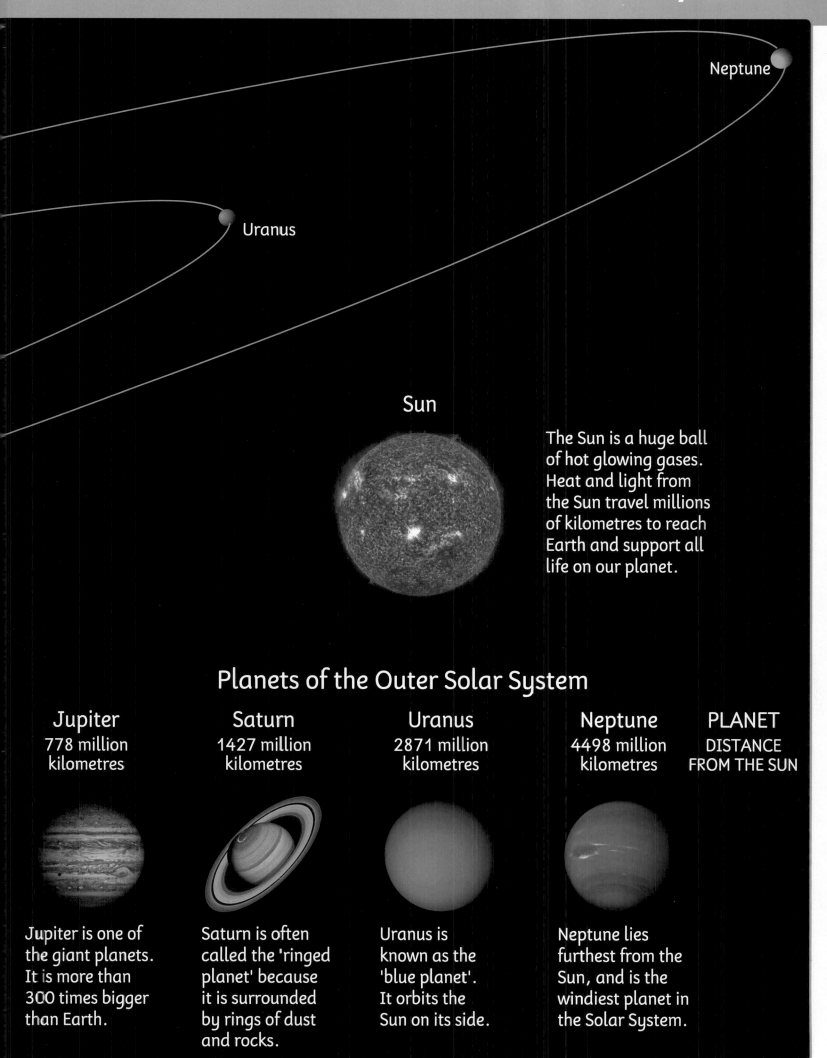

Neptune

Uranus

Sun

The Sun is a huge ball of hot glowing gases. Heat and light from the Sun travel millions of kilometres to reach Earth and support all life on our planet.

Planets of the Outer Solar System

Jupiter	Saturn	Uranus	Neptune	PLANET
778 million kilometres	1427 million kilometres	2871 million kilometres	4498 million kilometres	DISTANCE FROM THE SUN

Jupiter is one of the giant planets. It is more than 300 times bigger than Earth.

Saturn is often called the 'ringed planet' because it is surrounded by rings of dust and rocks.

Uranus is known as the 'blue planet'. It orbits the Sun on its side.

Neptune lies furthest from the Sun, and is the windiest planet in the Solar System.

The Moon

Only one side of the Moon is visible from Earth, the far side has only been seen by the few astronauts whose spaceships orbited it in the late 1960s and early 1970s.

Earth and its Moon compared

Plato

Mare Imbrium (Sea of Rains)

Montes Apeninus

Mare Serenitatis (Sea of Serenity)

Oceanus Procellarum (Ocean of Storms)

Copernicus

Mare Tranquillitatis (Sea of Tranquility)

● *Apollo 11 landing site (first men on the moon)*

Mare Nubium (Sea of Clouds)

Tycho

The phases of the Moon

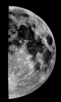

| New moon | Waxing crescent | First quarter | Waxing gibbous | Full moon | Waning gibbous | Last quarter | Waning crescent | New moon |

The new moon is not visible from Earth

The Seasons

The Earth's axis is tilted from perpendicular therefore different parts of the globe are oriented towards the Sun at different times of the year. The four seasons, Spring, Summer, Autumn and Winter are a result of this.

The Sun is overhead at the Equator and both the North and South poles are equidistant from the Sun. The Northern Hemisphere experiences Spring for three months while the Southern Hemisphere experiences Autumn.

March 21

The Sun is overhead at the Tropic of Capricorn. The North Pole is inclined away from the Sun and is in total darkness. The Northern Hemisphere experiences Winter for three months while the Southern Hemisphere experiences Summer.

December 21

Sun

September 21

The Sun is overhead at the Equator and both the North and South poles are equidistant from the Sun. The Northern Hemisphere experiences Autumn for three months while the Southern Hemisphere experiences Spring.

June 21

The Sun is overhead at the Tropic of Cancer. The North Pole is inclined towards the Sun and has 24 hour daylight. The Northern Hemisphere experiences Summer for three months while the Southern Hemisphere experiences Winter.

Day and Night

The Earth rotates on its axis every 24 hours. At any one moment in time one side of the Earth is in sunlight, while the other half is in darkness.

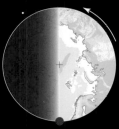 Dawn
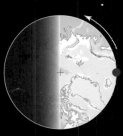 Midday
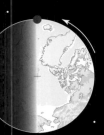 Dusk
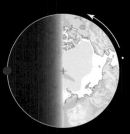 Midnight

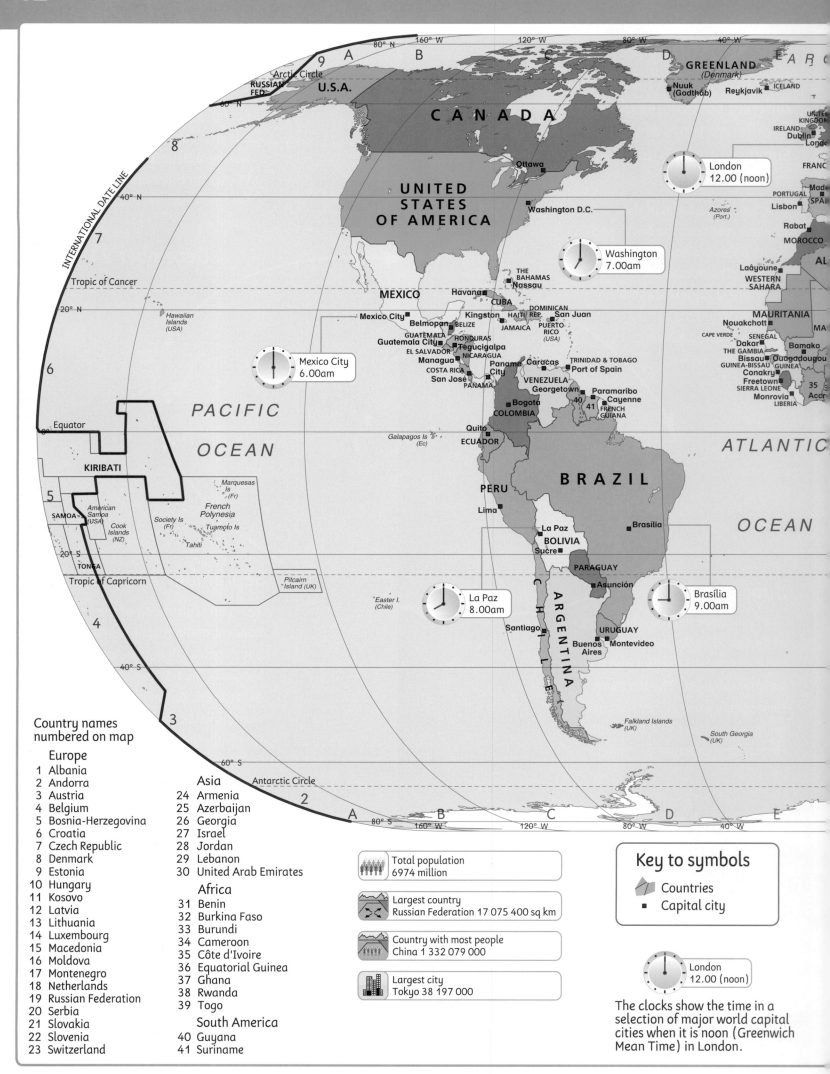

INTERNATIONAL DATE LINE

Arctic Circle

RUSSIAN FED.

U.S.A.

GREENLAND
(Denmark)

Nuuk
(Godthåb)

Reykjavik

ICELAND

CANADA

UNITED
KINGDOM

IRELAND
Dublin

FRANCE

London
12.00 (noon)

Ottawa

UNITED
STATES
OF AMERICA

Washington D.C.

PORTUGAL

Azores
(Port.)

Madeira

Lisbon

SPAIN

Rabat

MOROCCO

Washington
7.00am

Tropic of Cancer

THE
BAHAMAS
Nassau

Havana

MEXICO

CUBA

Mexico City

Kingston

JAMAICA

DOMINICAN
HAITI REP.

PUERTO
RICO
(USA)

San Juan

Laâyoune

WESTERN
SAHARA

MAURITANIA

ALG

MA

Nouakchott

Hawaiian
Islands
(USA)

GUATEMALA
Guatemala City

Belmopan

BELIZE

EL SALVADOR

Managua

HONDURAS
Tegucigalpa
NICARAGUA

CAPE VERDE

SENEGAL
Dakar
THE GAMBIA
Bissau
GUINEA-BISSAU
Conakry

Bamako

Ouagadougou

GUINEA

Mexico City
6.00am

COSTA RICA
San José

Panama
City

PANAMA

Caracas

Port of Spain

TRINIDAD & TOBAGO

SIERRA LEONE
Freetown
Monrovia
LIBERIA

Acc

35

VENEZUELA
Georgetown

Paramaribo
40 Cayenne
41 FRENCH
GUIANA

PACIFIC

Equator

Bogotá
COLOMBIA

Quito
ECUADOR

ATLANTIC

KIRIBATI

OCEAN

Galapagos Is
(Ec)

BRAZIL

OCEAN

Marquesas
Is
(Fr)

PERU

Lima

French
Polynesia

Society Is
(Fr)

American
Samoa
(USA)

Tuamoto Is

Cook
Islands
(NZ)

La Paz

Brasília

SAMOA

Tahiti

BOLIVIA
Sucre

TONGA

PARAGUAY

Tropic of Capricorn

Pitcairn
Island (UK)

Asunción

Brasília
9.00am

Easter I.
(Chile)

La Paz
8.00am

ARGENTINA

URUGUAY

Santiago

Buenos
Aires

Montevideo

Falkland Islands
(UK)

South Georgia
(UK)

Antarctic Circle

Country names
numbered on map

Europe
1 Albania
2 Andorra
3 Austria
4 Belgium
5 Bosnia-Herzegovina
6 Croatia
7 Czech Republic
8 Denmark
9 Estonia
10 Hungary
11 Kosovo
12 Latvia
13 Lithuania
14 Luxembourg
15 Macedonia
16 Moldova
17 Montenegro
18 Netherlands
19 Russian Federation
20 Serbia
21 Slovakia
22 Slovenia
23 Switzerland

Asia
24 Armenia
25 Azerbaijan
26 Georgia
27 Israel
28 Jordan
29 Lebanon
30 United Arab Emirates

Africa
31 Benin
32 Burkina Faso
33 Burundi
34 Cameroon
35 Côte d'Ivoire
36 Equatorial Guinea
37 Ghana
38 Rwanda
39 Togo

South America
40 Guyana
41 Suriname

Total population
6974 million

Largest country
Russian Federation 17 075 400 sq km

Country with most people
China 1 332 079 000

Largest city
Tokyo 38 197 000

Key to symbols

Countries

Capital city

London
12.00 (noon)

The clocks show the time in a
selection of major world capital
cities when it is noon (Greenwich
Mean Time) in London.

0 800 1600 2400 3200 km

Scale : One centimetre on this map is the same as 800 kilometres on the ground.

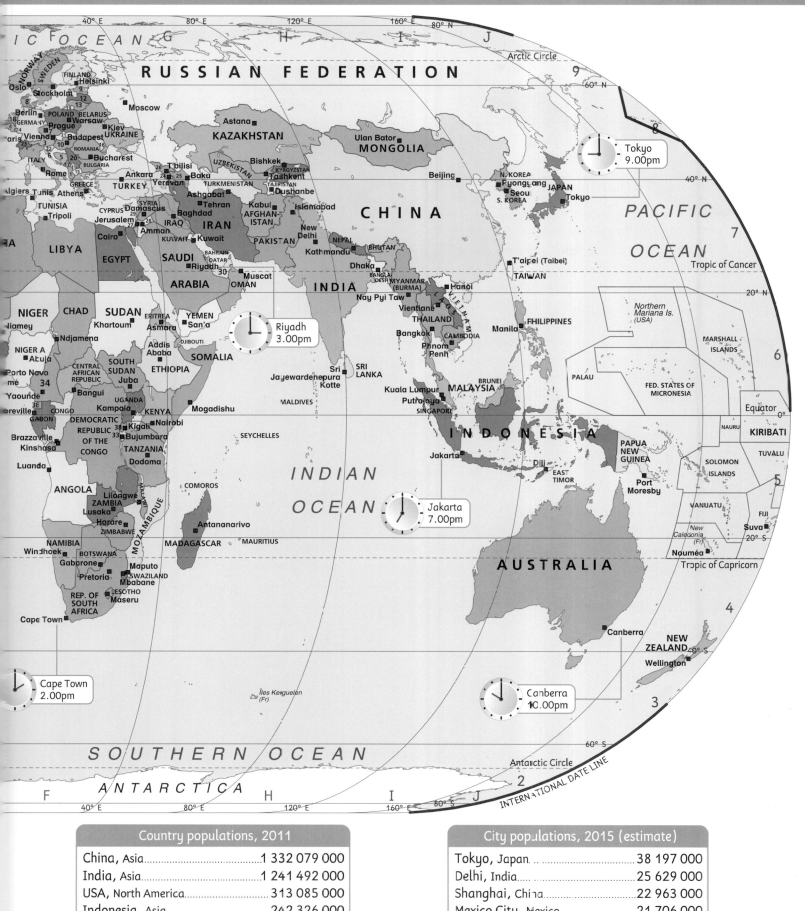

Country populations, 2011	
China, Asia	1 332 079 000
India, Asia	1 241 492 000
USA, North America	313 085 000
Indonesia, Asia	242 326 000
Brazil, South America	196 655 000
Pakistan, Asia	176 745 000
Nigeria, Africa	162 471 000
Bangladesh, Asia	150 494 000
Russian Federation, Asia/Europe	142 836 000
Japan, Asia	126 497 000

City populations, 2015 (estimate)	
Tokyo, Japan	38 197 000
Delhi, India	25 629 000
Shanghai, China	22 963 000
Mexico City, Mexico	21 706 000
New York, USA	21 326 000
Mumbai, India	21 214 000
São Paulo, Brazil	21 028 000
Beijing, China	18 079 000
Dhaka, Bangladesh	17 382 000
Karachi, Pakistan	15 500 000

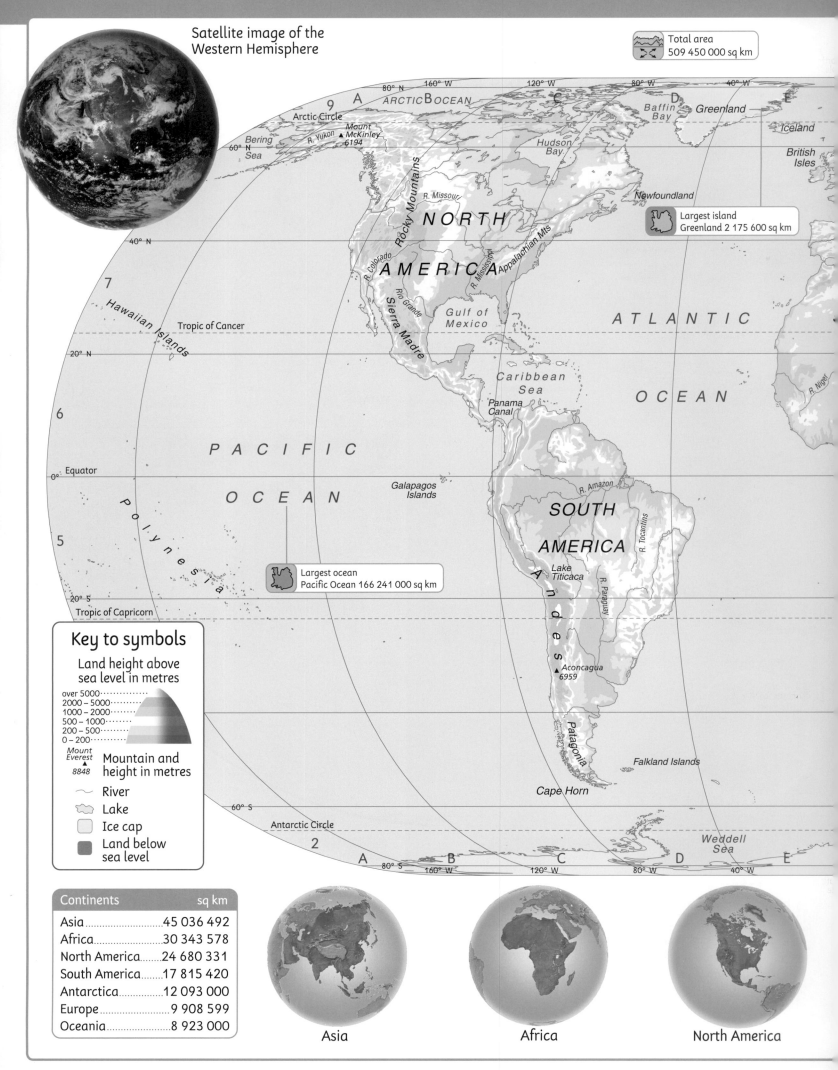

Satellite image of the
Western Hemisphere

Total area
509 450 000 sq km

Largest island
Greenland 2 175 600 sq km

Largest ocean
Pacific Ocean 166 241 000 sq km

ARCTIC OCEAN

Arctic Circle

Bering
Sea

R. Yukon

Mount
McKinley
6194

Baffin
Bay

Greenland

Iceland

British
Isles

Rocky Mountains

R. Missouri

Hudson
Bay

NORTH

AMERICA

R. Colorado

Appalachian Mts

R. Mississippi

Newfoundland

Sierra Madre

Rio Grande

Gulf of
Mexico

ATLANTIC

Hawaiian Islands

Tropic of Cancer

Caribbean
Sea

OCEAN

R. Niger

Panama
Canal

PACIFIC

Galapagos
Islands

R. Amazon

OCEAN

SOUTH

Equator

Polynesia

AMERICA

R. Tocantins

Andes

Lake
Titicaca

R. Paraguay

Tropic of Capricorn

Aconcagua
6959

Key to symbols

Land height above
sea level in metres

over 5000
2000 – 5000
1000 – 2000
500 – 1000
200 – 500
0 – 200

Mount
Everest ▲
8848

Mountain and
height in metres

⌒ River

🗺 Lake

☐ Ice cap

■ Land below
sea level

Patagonia

Falkland Islands

Cape Horn

Antarctic Circle

Weddell
Sea

Continents	sq km
Asia	45 036 492
Africa	30 343 578
North America	24 680 331
South America	17 815 420
Antarctica	12 093 000
Europe	9 908 599
Oceania	8 923 000

Asia

Africa

North America

0   800   1600   2400   3200 km

Scale : One centimetre on this map is the same as 800 kilometres on the ground.

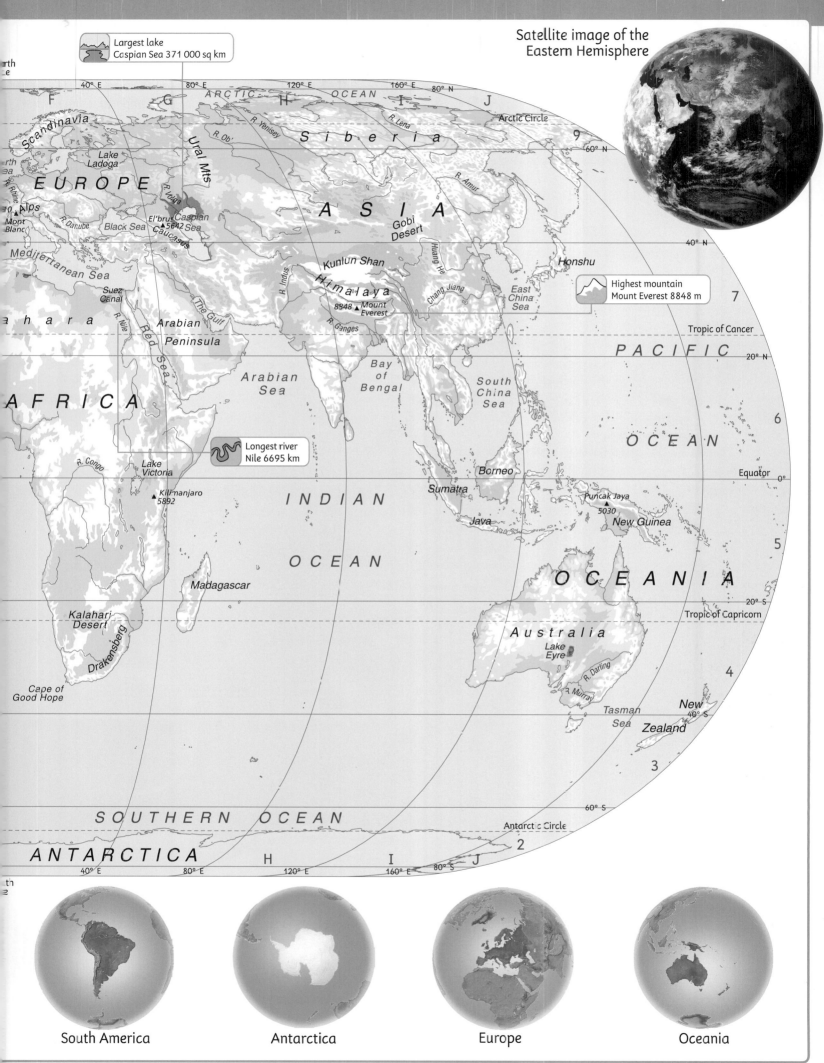

Satellite image of the
Eastern Hemisphere

Largest lake
Caspian Sea 371 000 sq km

Highest mountain
Mount Everest 8848 m

Longest river
Nile 6695 km

ARCTIC OCEAN

40° E   80° E   120° E   160° E   80° N

Arctic Circle

Scandinavia

S i b e r i a

9

R. Yenisey
R. Lena
R. Ob

60° N

Lake
Ladoga

E U R O P E

A S I A

R. Amur

Ural Mts

Caspian
Sea

R. Volga

El'brus
5642
Caucasus

Gobi
Desert

40° N

Alps
Mont
Blanc

R. Danube

Black Sea

Rhine

Mediterranean Sea

Kunlun Shan

Honshu

Himalaya

Huang He

East
China
Sea

7

Suez
Canal

R. Indus

8848   Mount
Everest

Chang Jiang

Sahara

The Gulf

Arabian
Peninsula

R. Nile

Red Sea

R. Ganges

Tropic of Cancer

20° N

A F R I C A

Arabian
Sea

Bay
of
Bengal

South
China
Sea

P A C I F I C

O C E A N

6

R. Congo

Lake
Victoria

Borneo

Equator   0°

Kilimanjaro
5892

Sumatra

Puncak Jaya
5030

Java

New Guinea

I N D I A N

O C E A N

5

Madagascar

O C E A N I A

20° S

Kalahari
Desert

Tropic of Capricorn

Australia

Drakensberg

Lake
Eyre

Cape of
Good Hope

R. Darling

4

R. Murray

Tasman
Sea

New
Zealand   40° S

3

S O U T H E R N   O C E A N

60° S

Antarctic Circle

A N T A R C T I C A

2

40° E   80° E   120° E   160° E   80° S

South America   Antarctica   Europe   Oceania

Key to symbols
Countries
■ Capital city
○ Important city/town

Total population of Europe
(excluding Russian Federation)
596 million

Russian Federation
Area 17 075 400 sq km
Population 142 836 000

ARCTIC OCEAN

Spitsbergen

Novaya
Zemlya

Jan Mayen
(Norway)

ATLANTIC
OCEAN

Faroe Islands
(Denmark)

White Sea

RUSSIAN
FEDERATION

ICELAND
Reykjavík

Country with most people
(excluding Russian Federation)
Germany 82 163 000

NORWAY
SWEDEN
FINLAND

Oslo
Stockholm
Helsinki
St Petersburg

Tallinn
ESTONIA
LATVIA
Riga
LITHUANIA
Vilnius
Minsk

Moscow

Edinburgh
Belfast
Dublin
IRELAND
UNITED
KINGDOM
London

North
Sea

DENMARK
Copenhagen

Baltic Sea

8

BELARUS

Largest country
(excluding Russian Federation)
Ukraine 603 700 sq km

Volgograd

Amsterdam
The
Hague 7
Brussels 1
5

Berlin
GERMANY

Warsaw
POLAND

Kiev

UKRAINE

English Channel

Paris

Prague
CZECH REPUBLIC
SLOVAKIA

MOLDOVA
Chişinău

Caspian
Sea

Largest city
(Western Europe)
Paris 11 097 000

FRANCE

Munich
Vienna
Bern
10 4
AUSTRIA
Bratislava
Budapest
HUNGARY

Odesa

Lyon

Ljubljana 9
Zagreb
CROATIA

ROMANIA
Belgrade
Bucharest

Bay of
Biscay

Milan
SAN
MARINO
Sarajevo
2
SERBIA

Black Sea

MONACO
ITALY
Adriatic Sea
6 3
Skopje
MACEDONIA

BULGARIA
Sofia

PORTUGAL
ANDORRA

Corsica

Istanbul

Largest city
Istanbul 12 459 000

Lisbon
Madrid
SPAIN
Barcelona
Balearic
Islands

Rome
Tirana
ALBANIA

TURKEY

ASIA

Sardinia

GREECE
Aegean
Sea

Gibraltar (UK)
Strait of
Gibraltar

Mediterranean

Sicily

Athens

Rhodes

Sea

Crete

AFRICA

MALTA

1 BELGIUM
2 BOSNIA-HERZEGOVINA
3 KOSOVO
4 LIECHTENSTEIN
5 LUXEMBOURG
6 MONTENEGRO
7 NETHERLANDS
8 RUSSIAN FEDERATION
9 SLOVENIA
10 SWITZERLAND

Other maps showing regions
of Europe are on pages:
25 Ireland
26-27 Northern Europe
28-29 Southern Europe
25 26-27
28-29

The Colosseum, an ancient Roman sports arena, was
once used for gladiator fights.

The Eiffel Tower in France's
capital city, Paris.

0 250 500 750 1000 1250 km

Scale : One centimetre on this map is the same as 250 kilometres on the ground.

Total area of Europe
9 908 599 sq km

Greenland

Spitsbergen

Novaya
Zemlya

ARCTIC OCEAN

ASIA

Jan
Mayen

North Cape

Iceland

Largest island
Great Britain 218 476 sq km

Lofoten Is

Kola
Peninsula

Lappland

White Sea

R. Pechora

Ural Mountains

ATLANTIC

Faroe Islands

Scandinavia

Gulf of Bothnia

Lake
Onega

R. Northern Dvina

R. Sukhona

OCEAN

Shetland Islands

Lake
Ladoga

R. Volga

Orkney Islands

Vänern

Lake
Peipus

Volga
Uplands

British
Isles

North
Sea

Vättern

Longest river
Volga 3688 km

Great Britain

Jutland

Baltic Sea

North European Plain

R. Dvina

Central Russian Uplands

Caspian
Lowland

Ireland

R. Elbe

R. Vistula

R. Volga

R. Thames

R. Rhine

R. Oder

R. Don

R. Donets

English Channel

R. Seine

Sudeten Mts

R. Dniester

R. Dnieper

Caspian Sea

R. Loire

Carpathian Mountains

R. Danube

R. Don

Bay
of
Biscay

Jura

Alps

Hungarian
Plain

Black Sea

Caucasus

El'brus
5642

Massif
Central

Mont Blanc
4810

R. Rhône

Largest lake
Caspian Sea 371 000 sq km

Cape
Finisterre

Cantabrian Mts

Pyrenees

R. Po

Dinaric Alps

R. Danube

R. Duero

R. Ebro

3404

Adriatic Sea

Apennines

Balkan Mts

Iberian

Corsica

Peninsula

R. Tagus

Balearic
Islands

Sardinia

Pindus Mts

Aegean
Sea

ASIA

Cape
St Vincent

Sierra Nevada

Mediterranean

Highest mountain
El'brus 5642 m

Strait of
Gibraltar

Mount Etna
Sicily
3323

Sea

Rhodes

Malta

Crete

AFRICA

Mount Etna, on the island of Sicily, is
one of the world's most active volcanoes.

Narrow, steep sided inlets called fjords are found
along much of the Norwegian coastline.

Key to symbols

**Land height above
sea level in metres**

over 5000
2000 – 5000
1000 – 2000
500 – 1000
200 – 500
0 – 200

El'brus
5642 ▲ Mountain and
height in metres

⌒ River

Lake

Seasonal lake

Ice cap

Land below
sea level

0 250 500 750 1000 1250 km

Scale : One centimetre on this map is the same as 250 kilometres on the ground.

European Union

The European Union (EU) was created in 1957 by the Treaty of Rome. The original members of the then European Economic Community (EEC) were Belgium, France, West Germany, Italy, Luxembourg and the Netherlands. Since 1957 the EU has grown and now has 27 member states. The total population of the EU is now nearly half a billion.

The headquarters of the EU in the Belgian capital, Brussels.

ICELAND

NORWAY

SWEDEN

FINLAND

ESTONIA

LATVIA

LITHUANIA

R.F.

DENMARK

UNITED KINGDOM

IRELAND

NETHERLANDS

BELARUS

POLAND

GERMANY

BELGIUM

LUX.

CZECH REPUBLIC

SLOVAKIA

UKRAINE

FRANCE

SWITZ.

L.

AUSTRIA

HUNGARY

MOL.

SL.

CROATIA

ROMANIA

B.-H.

SERBIA

MON.

KOS.

MAC.

BULGARIA

ALBANIA

PORTUGAL

ANDORRA

SPAIN

ITALY

GREECE

TURKEY

MALTA

CYPRUS

Legend:
- EU member
- EU applicant
- Non EU member

B.-H. BOSNIA-HERZEGOVINA
KOS. KOSOVO
L. LIECHTENSTEIN
LUX. LUXEMBOURG
MAC. MACEDONIA
MOL. MOLDOVA
MON. MONTENEGRO
R.F. RUSSIAN FEDERATION
SL. SLOVENIA
SWITZ. SWITZERLAND

Flags:

Austria | Denmark | Greece | Lithuania | Poland | Slovenia
Belgium | Estonia | Hungary | Luxembourg | Portugal | Spain
Bulgaria | Finland | Ireland | Malta | Romania | Sweden
Cyprus | France | Italy | Netherlands | Slovakia | United Kingdom
Czech Republic | Germany | Latvia

Key to symbols

◤ Countries
■ Capital city
○ Important city/town

Other maps showing regions of the United Kingdom are on pages:
22-23 England and Wales
24 Scotland
25 Northern Ireland

N
W E
S

Shetland Islands

Orkney Islands

Outer Hebrides

ATLANTIC OCEAN

Inverness

Aberdeen

Fort William

SCOTLAND

Dundee

North Sea

Glasgow ○ ■ **Edinburgh**

Londonderry

NORTHERN IRELAND ■ **Belfast**

Newcastle upon Tyne

Middlesbrough

UNITED

Dundalk

Isle of Man

York

IRELAND

Irish Sea

Blackpool Bradford Leeds
Preston

KINGDOM

Manchester
Sheffield

Galway

Liverpool

Dublin ■

Stoke-on-Trent Derby Nottingham

ENGLAND

Norwich

Limerick

WALES

Wolverhampton Leicester
Birmingham
Coventry

Cambridge
Ipswich

Waterford

Cork

Oxford

London ■ Southend-on-Sea

Celtic Sea

Swansea

Cardiff ■

Bristol Reading

BELGIUM

Southampton
Portsmouth
Bournemouth

Brighton

Plymouth Torquay

English Channel

Channel Islands

FRANCE

Tower Bridge crosses the River Thames in London.

0   50   100   150   200   250 km

Scale : One centimetre on this map is the same as 50 kilometres on the ground.

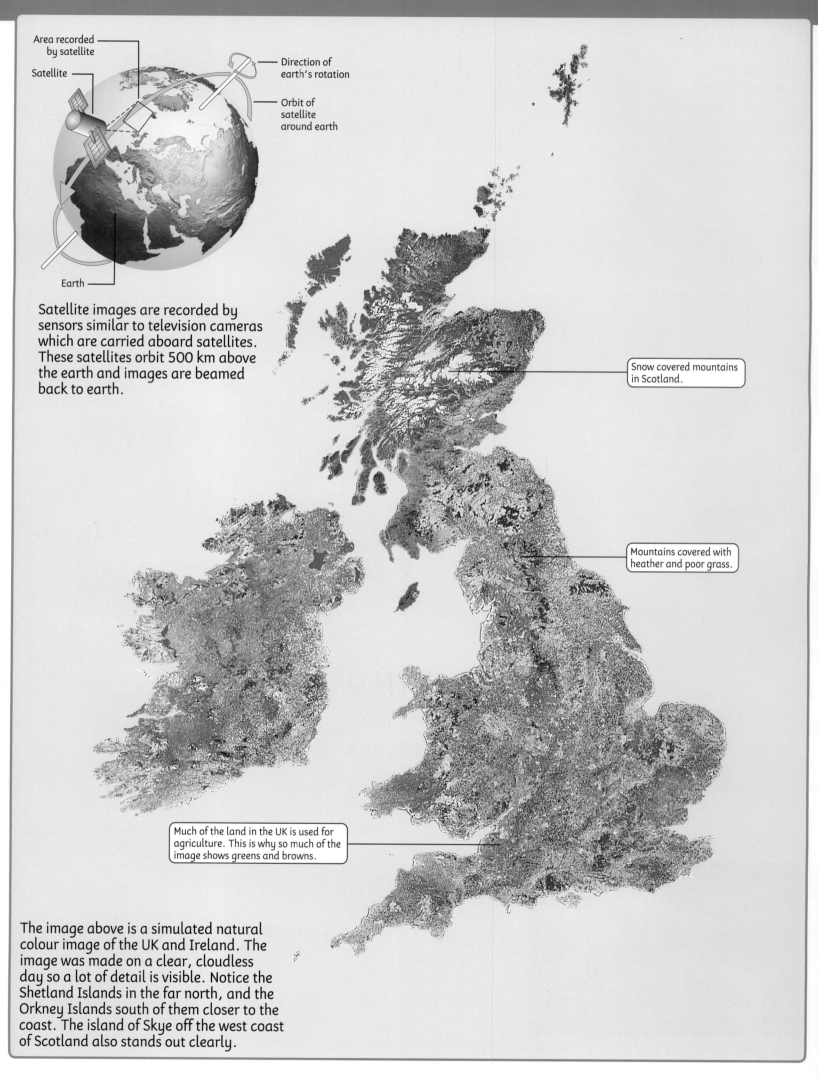

Area recorded by satellite

Satellite

Direction of earth's rotation

Orbit of satellite around earth

Earth

Satellite images are recorded by sensors similar to television cameras which are carried aboard satellites. These satellites orbit 500 km above the earth and images are beamed back to earth.

Snow covered mountains in Scotland.

Mountains covered with heather and poor grass.

Much of the land in the UK is used for agriculture. This is why so much of the image shows greens and browns.

The image above is a simulated natural colour image of the UK and Ireland. The image was made on a clear, cloudless day so a lot of detail is visible. Notice the Shetland Islands in the far north, and the Orkney Islands south of them closer to the coast. The island of Skye off the west coast of Scotland also stands out clearly.

Key to symbols

Land height above sea level in metres

over 1000
500 – 1000
200 – 500
100 – 200
0 – 100

Ben Nevis ▲ 1344 Mountain and height in metres

River

Lake

Land below sea level

Total area of the United Kingdom
243 609 sq km

Highest mountain
Ben Nevis 1344 m

One of Scotland's famous glens, Glencoe.

Largest lake
Lough Neagh 396 sq km

Largest island
Great Britain 218 476 sq km

Longest river
River Severn 354 km

N
W E
S

Shetland Islands
Mainland
Sumburgh Head

Orkney Islands
Mainland
Hoy
Pentland Firth
Duncansby Head

Cape Wrath

Outer Hebrides
Isle of Lewis
Harris
St Kilda
North Uist
Skye
South Uist
Inner Hebrides
Rum
Coll
Tiree
Ben More 966
Mull
Jura
Islay
Arran

The Minch

North West Highlands

Loch Ness
R. Spey
Cairngorm Mts
Ben Macdui 1309
R. Dee
Ben Nevis 1344
Grampian Mts
Glen Coe
Loch Tay
R. Tay
Ochil Hills
Loch Lomond
R. Forth
Firth of Forth
R. Clyde
Firth of Clyde

Moray Firth

ATLANTIC OCEAN

North Sea

Malin Head
Donegal Bay
Achill
Lough Mask
Lough Corrib
Galway Bay
R. Shannon
Lough Ree
Lough Derg
R. Suir
Carrantuohill 1041
R. Blackwater
Cape Clear

R. Foyle
Lower Lough Erne
Upper Lough Erne
Antrim Hills
R. Bann
Lough Neagh
Mourne Mts
Slieve Donard 852
Dundalk Bay
R. Boyne
R. Barrow
Lugnaquilla Mtn 926
Wicklow Mts

Ireland

North Channel

Isle of Man

Irish Sea

Southern Uplands
Merrick 843
R. Tweed
Cheviot Hills
R. Tyne
Solway Firth
Scafell Pike 977
Lake District
R. Tees
North York Moors
Flamborough Head
R. Ouse
Spurn Head

Great Britain

Pennines

High Peak
R. Mersey
Kinder Scout 636
R. Trent
The Wash

Anglesey
Snowdon 1085
Cambrian Mountains
R. Dee
R. Severn
Black Mountains 886
Brecon Beacons
R. Wye
R. Severn
Cotswold Hills
R. Avon
R. Great Ouse
The Fens
Norfolk Broads
Chiltern Hills
R. Thames
R. Thames
North Downs
South Downs
Beachy Head

Cardigan Bay
St George's Channel
St David's Head

Celtic Sea

Bristol Channel
Exmoor
Mendip Hills
Isle of Wight

Dartmoor
Yes Tor 619
R. Taw
Lyme Bay
Bodmin Moor
Land's End
Start Point
Isles of Scilly

English Channel

Channel Islands

The South Downs drop down to the sea in chalk cliffs at Beachy Head.

0 50 100 150 200 250 km

Scale : One centimetre on this map is the same as 50 kilometres on the ground.

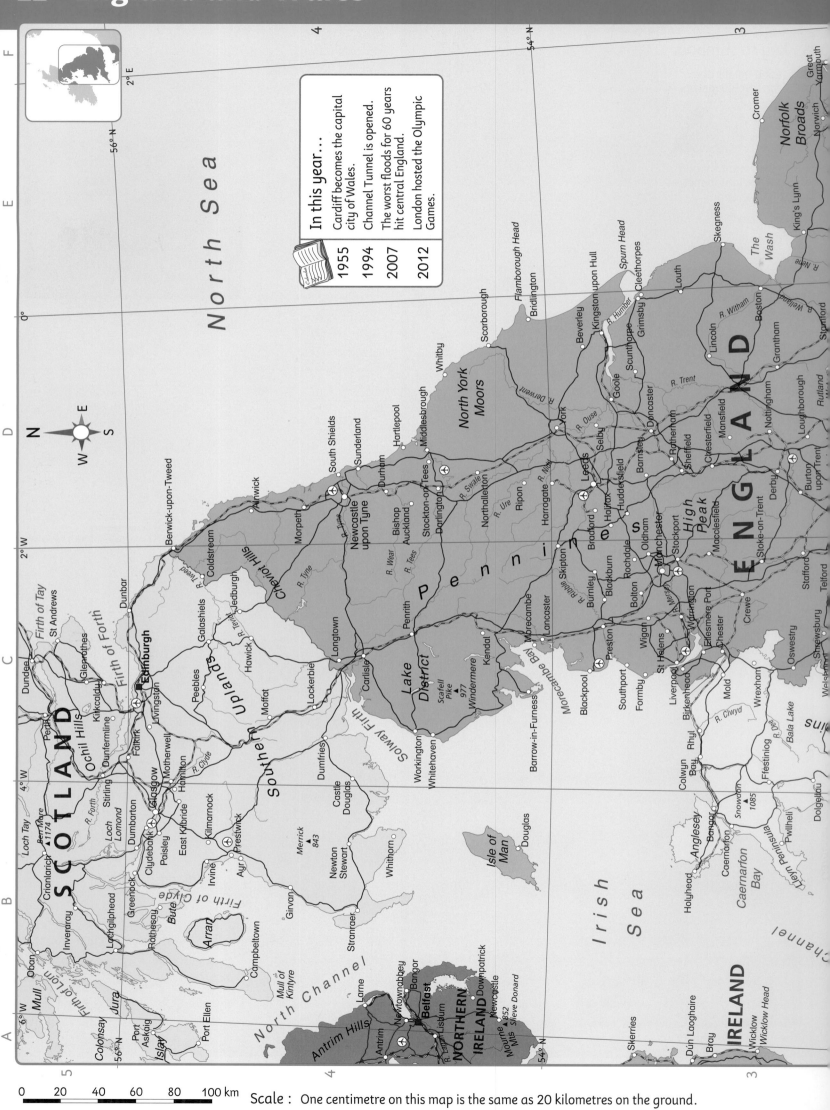

F

E

D

C

B

A

4

3

2° E

56° N

54° N

0°

2° W

4° W

6° W

56° N

54° N

In this year…

1955 — Cardiff becomes the capital city of Wales.
1994 — Channel Tunnel is opened.
2007 — The worst floods for 60 years hit central England.
2012 — London hosted the Olympic Games.

North Sea

Irish Sea

North Channel

N
W — E
S

SCOTLAND

ENGLAND

IRELAND

NORTHERN IRELAND

Pennines

Southern Uplands

Cheviot Hills

Lake District

North York Moors

High Peak

Norfolk Broads

Firth of Tay
Firth of Forth
Firth of Clyde
Solway Firth
Morecambe Bay
Caernarfon Bay
Colwyn Bay
The Wash

Isle of Man

Anglesey

Llŷn Peninsula

Ochil Hills

Antrim Hills

Oban
Inveraray
Lochgilphead
Crianlarich ▲1174
Ben More
Loch Tay
Mull
Colonsay
Jura
Islay
Port Askaig
Port Ellen
Campbeltown
Mull of Kintyre
Arran
Bute
Rothesay
Greenock
Dumbarton
Clydebank
Paisley
Glasgow
East Kilbride
Hamilton
Motherwell
R. Clyde
Loch Lomond
Kilmarnock
Irvine
Prestwick
Ayr
Girvan
Loch Fyne
R. Forth
Stirling
Falkirk
Livingston
Dunfermline
Kirkcaldy
Perth
Dundee
St Andrews
Glenrothes
Edinburgh
Peebles
Galashiels
Hawick
Jedburgh
R. Teviot
R. Tweed
Moffat
Lockerbie
Dumfries
Castle Douglas
Newton Stewart
Merrick 843
Whithorn
Stranraer
Douglas
Larne
Newtownabbey
Bangor
Belfast
Lisburn
Downpatrick
Newcastle
Mourne
Slieve Donard ▲852
Antrim
R. Lagan
Sherries
Dún Laoghaire
Bray
Wicklow
Wicklow Head
Holyhead
Caernarfon
Bangor
Snowdon ▲1085
R. Clwyd
Rhyl
Colwyn Bay
Mold
Wrexham
R. Dee
Bala Lake
Dolgellau
Ffestiniog
Pwllheli
Oswestry
Shrewsbury
Telford
Stafford
Stoke-on-Trent
Crewe
Chester
Ellesmere Port
Birkenhead
Liverpool
St Helens
Warrington
Wigan
Bolton
Rochdale
Oldham
Manchester
Stockport
Macclesfield
Southport
Formby
Blackpool
Preston
Blackburn
Burnley
R. Ribble
Skipton
Lancaster
Morecambe
Barrow-in-Furness
Workington
Whitehaven
Scafell Pike ▲977
Windermere
Kendal
Penrith
Carlisle
Longtown
Coldstream
Berwick-upon-Tweed
Alnwick
Morpeth
Newcastle upon Tyne
R. Tyne
Bishop Auckland
Durham
Sunderland
South Shields
Hartlepool
Middlesbrough
Stockton-on-Tees
Darlington
R. Tees
R. Wear
Whitby
Scarborough
Northallerton
R. Swale
R. Ure
Ripon
Harrogate
Leeds
Bradford
Halifax
Huddersfield
Barnsley
Wakefield
Sheffield
Rotherham
Chesterfield
Mansfield
Derby
Burton upon Trent
Stone
Stoke-on-Trent
R. Nidd
York
R. Ouse
R. Derwent
Selby
Goole
Doncaster
Scunthorpe
Kingston upon Hull
Beverley
Bridlington
Flamborough Head
Spurn Head
Cleethorpes
Grimsby
Louth
Skegness
Boston
Lincoln
R. Witham
R. Trent
Nottingham
Loughborough
Grantham
Rutland
Stamford
R. Nene
R. Welland
King's Lynn
Norwich
Great Yarmouth
Cromer

0   20   40   60   80   100 km

Scale : One centimetre on this map is the same as 20 kilometres on the ground.

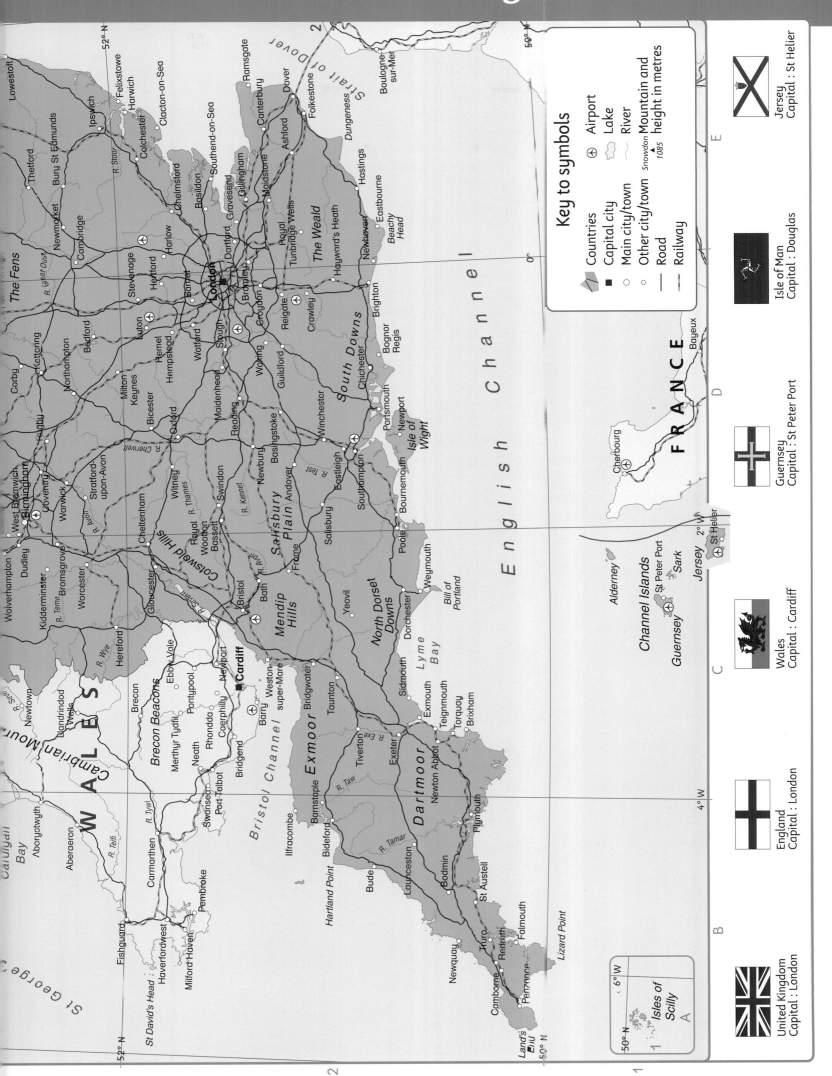

Key to symbols

Countries	Airport
Capital city	Lake
Main city/town	River
Other city/town	Snowdon Mountain and
Road	1085 height in metres
Railway	

United Kingdom
Capital : London

England
Capital : London

Wales
Capital : Cardiff

Guernsey
Capital : St Peter Port

Isle of Man
Capital : Douglas

Jersey
Capital : St Helier

Isles of Scilly

FRANCE

English Channel

Strait of Dover

The Weald

South Downs

WALES

Cambrian Mountains

Brecon Beacons

Cotswold Hills

Salisbury Plain

Mendip Hills

North Dorset Downs

Exmoor

Dartmoor

The Fens

Channel Islands
Alderney
Guernsey St Peter Port Sark
Jersey St Helier

Cherbourg
Bayeux

St George's Channel
Cardigan Bay
Bristol Channel
Lyme Bay
Bill of Portland
Beachy Head
Dungeness
Hartland Point
Lizard Point
Land's End
St David's Head

London (Capital)
Cardiff (Capital)

Lowestoft, Felixstowe, Harwich, Ipswich, Clacton-on-Sea, Colchester, Thetford, Bury St Edmunds, Newmarket, Cambridge, Bedford, Kettering, Corby, Northampton, Milton Keynes, Bicester, Oxford, Luton, Stevenage, Hertford, Harlow, Basildon, Chelmsford, Southend-on-Sea, Gravesend, Dartford, Bromley, Croydon, Gillingham, Maidstone, Royal Tunbridge Wells, Hayward's Heath, Brighton, Newhaven, Eastbourne, Hastings, Ashford, Canterbury, Ramsgate, Dover, Folkestone, Boulogne-sur-Mer

Birmingham, West Bromwich, Coventry, Warwick, Stratford-upon-Avon, Bromsgrove, Worcester, Kidderminster, Dudley, Wolverhampton, Rugby, Hereford, Gloucester, Cheltenham, Witney, Royal Wootton Bassett, Swindon, Newbury, Reading, Maidenhead, Slough, Watford, Woking, Guildford, Reigate, Crawley, Andover, Basingstoke, Winchester, Chichester, Bognor Regis, Portsmouth, Southampton, Eastleigh, Isle of Wight, Newport, Bournemouth, Poole, Weymouth, Dorchester, Yeovil, Salisbury, Frome, Bath, Bristol, Weston-super-Mare, Bridgwater, Taunton, Tiverton, Exeter, Newton Abbot, Teignmouth, Torquay, Brixham, Exmouth, Sidmouth, Plymouth, Bodmin, St Austell, Newquay, Truro, Redruth, Camborne, Penzance, Falmouth, Bude, Launceston, Bideford, Barnstaple, Ilfracombe

Newport, Cardiff, Barry, Bridgend, Port Talbot, Swansea, Neath, Caerphilly, Rhondda, Merthyr Tydfil, Pontypool, Ebbw Vale, Pontypridd, Brecon, Builth Wells, Llandrindod Wells, Newtown, Aberystwyth, Aberaeron, Carmarthen, Pembroke, Milford Haven, Haverfordwest, Fishguard, St David's Head

Rivers: R. Stour, R. Great Ouse, R. Cherwell, R. Thames, R. Kennet, R. Test, R. Avon, R. Teme, R. Wye, R. Severn, R. Exe, R. Taw, R. Tamar, R. Tywi, R. Teifi, R. Severn

50° N
52° N
0°
4° W
6° W
2° W

Scotland
Capital : Edinburgh

In this year…

1975 — First oil is piped ashore from the North Sea.

1995 — Skye road bridge is opened.

2003 — The Cairngorms becomes Scotland's second National Park.

2010 — Scotland sees the worst snow fall for 30 years.

Key to symbols

- Countries
- Capital city
- Main city/town
- Other city/town
- Road
- Railway
- Airport
- Lake
- River
- *Ben Nevis* 1344 Mountain and height in metres

Scale : One centimetre on this map is the same as 20 kilometres on the ground.

0 20 40 60 80 100 km

Key to symbols

- Countries
- ■ Capital city
- ○ Main city/town
- ○ Other city/town
- — Road
- ⊢⊢ Railway
- ⊕ Airport
- Lake
- River
- *Carrantuohill* ▲ Mountain and
  1041 height in metres

SCOTLAND

Port Askaig *Jura*
Islay Rothesay *Bute*
Port Ellen *Arran* Irvine
Campbeltown Prestwick
Mull of Ayr
Kintyre Girvan
Stranraer

Malin Head

Bloody Foreland

Errigal
▲ 752

Letterkenny

Portrush
Lough Coleraine
Foyle Antrim Hills
Londonderry R. Bann
Strabane Ballymena Larne
North Channel

Donegal

NORTHERN

Omagh Cookstown Antrim Newtownabbey
Lower Lough Bangor
Lough Neagh Belfast
Erne Dungannon Lisburn
R. Lagan Downpatrick

Donegal Bay

Erris Head
Belmullet

Sligo Enniskillen
Upper Armagh Newry Newcastle
Lough Monaghan ▲ 852 *Isle of*
Erne Slieve Donard *Man*
Mourne
Mts

Ballina

*Lough
Conn*

54° N Carrick-on- Cavan Dundalk 54° N
Shannon *Dundalk Bay*

Achill
Island Castlebar Charlestown

Westport Lough Claremorris Longford Drogheda
Mask Roscommon *Lough* Novan Skerries
Ree
Lough R. Suck Mullingar R. Boyne
Corrib Athlone
Connemara

Galway Tullamore *Dublin*
Dún Laoghaire
Galway Bay **IRELAND** R. Liffey Bray
Naas Wicklow Mts

Aran Lough R. Shannon Portlaoise Wicklow
Islands Derg Roscrea Wicklow Head

**ATLANTIC
OCEAN** Ennis Nenagh R. Barrow Carlow Arklow

Kilkee R. Nore Enniscorthy
Kilrush Thurles Kilkenny
Limerick R. Suir New Ross Wexford
Tipperary Carrick- Rosslare
Cahir on-Suir
Tralee Clonmel
Dingle Knockmealdown Mts Waterford
Killarney Mallow R. Blackwater Fermoy Dungarvan Fishguard
Carrantuohill Youghal **WALES**
▲ Boggeragh Mts St David's Head
1041 R. Lee Haverfordwest
52° N Dingle Bay Sneem Cork Milford Haven
Cobh Pembroke
Bantry
Skibbereen
Mizen Head Cape Clear Old Head
of Kinsale
Celtic
Sea

*Irish
Sea*

St George's Channel

In this year...

1920	Ireland becomes an independent country.
2002	Ireland adopts the euro as its currency.
2005	Ireland's first offshore wind farm is switched on at Arklow Bank.

Ireland
Capital : Dublin

Northern Ireland
Capital : Belfast

0 20 40 60 80 100 km

Scale : One centimetre on this map is the same as 20 kilometres on the ground.

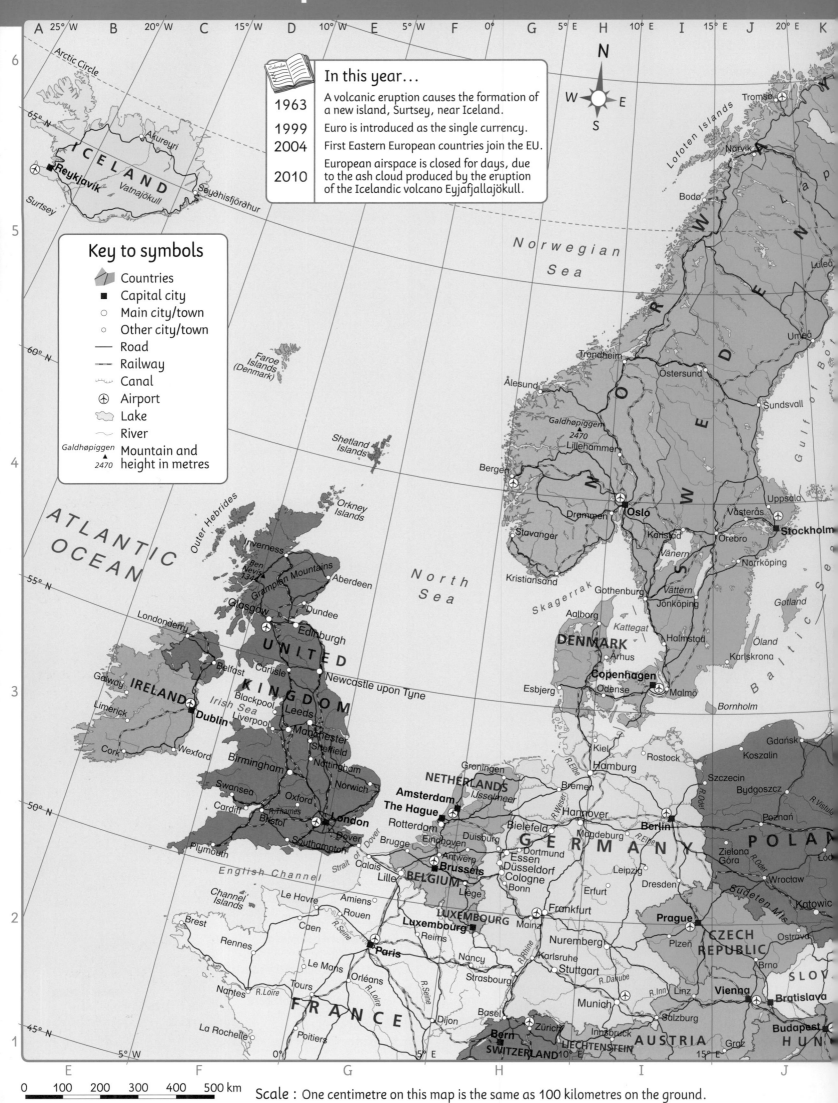

In this year...

1963   A volcanic eruption causes the formation of a new island, Surtsey, near Iceland.

1999   Euro is introduced as the single currency.

2004   First Eastern European countries join the EU.

2010   European airspace is closed for days, due to the ash cloud produced by the eruption of the Icelandic volcano Eyjafjallajökull.

Key to symbols

- Countries
- ■ Capital city
- ○ Main city/town
- ○ Other city/town
- Road
- Railway
- Canal
- ✈ Airport
- Lake
- River
- *Galdhøpiggen* ▲ Mountain and height in metres
  2470

Scale : One centimetre on this map is the same as 100 kilometres on the ground.

0 100 200 300 400 500 km

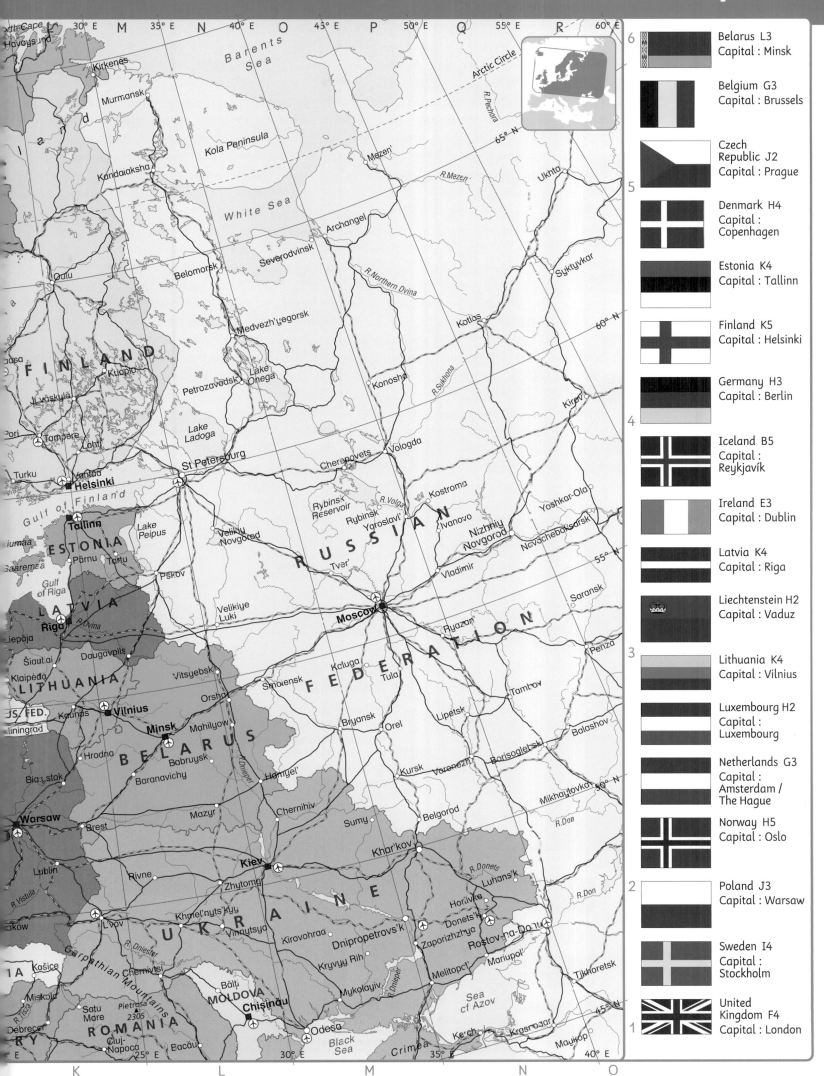

Belarus L3
Capital : Minsk

Belgium G3
Capital : Brussels

Czech Republic J2
Capital : Prague

Denmark H4
Capital : Copenhagen

Estonia K4
Capital : Tallinn

Finland K5
Capital : Helsinki

Germany H3
Capital : Berlin

Iceland B5
Capital : Reykjavík

Ireland E3
Capital : Dublin

Latvia K4
Capital : Riga

Liechtenstein H2
Capital : Vaduz

Lithuania K4
Capital : Vilnius

Luxembourg H2
Capital : Luxembourg

Netherlands G3
Capital : Amsterdam / The Hague

Norway H5
Capital : Oslo

Poland J3
Capital : Warsaw

Sweden I4
Capital : Stockholm

United Kingdom F4
Capital : London

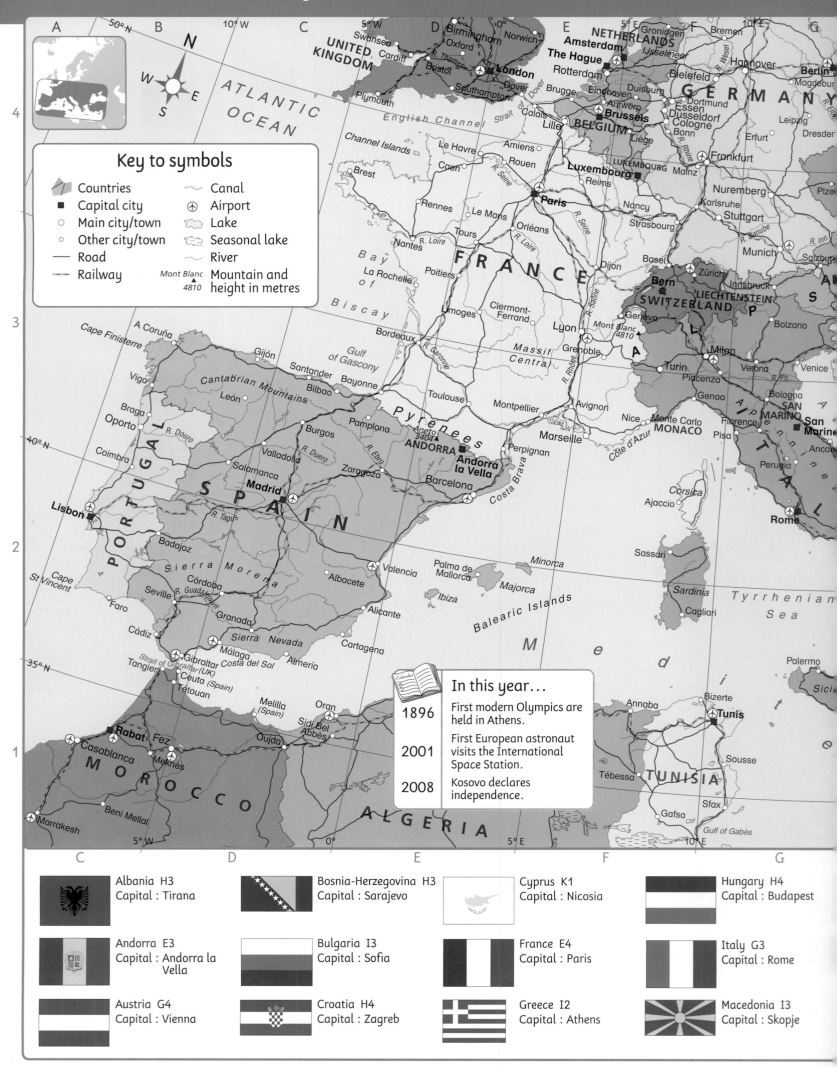

Key to symbols

- ◤ Countries
- ■ Capital city
- ○ Main city/town
- ○ Other city/town
- — Road
- ⊨ Railway
- ⌇ Canal
- ⊕ Airport
- ⬭ Lake
- ⬭ Seasonal lake
- ～ River
- *Mont Blanc* ▲ Mountain and
- 4810 height in metres

ATLANTIC OCEAN

UNITED KINGDOM
Swansea, Cardiff, Bristol, London, Plymouth, Southampton, Dover, Birmingham, Oxford, Norwich
English Channel

NETHERLANDS
Amsterdam, The Hague, Rotterdam, Groningen, Ijsselmeer
GERMANY
Bremen, Hannover, Berlin, Magdeburg, Bielefeld, Dortmund, Essen, Düsseldorf, Cologne, Bonn, Leipzig, Erfurt, Dresden, Frankfurt, Mainz, Nuremberg, Karlsruhe, Stuttgart, Munich, Salzburg
BELGIUM
Brussels, Brugge, Antwerp, Eindhoven, Duisburg, Liège
Lille, Calais, Le Havre, Amiens, Rouen, Caen, Reims, Nancy
LUXEMBOURG
Luxembourg
Paris
Brest, Rennes, Le Mans, Tours, Orléans, Nantes
R. Loire
R. Seine
FRANCE
Limoges, Clermont-Ferrand, Lyon, Dijon, Basel, Geneva, Grenoble
Massif Central
Bay of Biscay
La Rochelle, Poitiers, Bordeaux
R. Garonne
Gulf of Gascony
Mont Blanc 4810
SWITZERLAND
Bern, Zürich, Innsbruck
LIECHTENSTEIN
Milan, Turin, Verona, Venice, Bolzano, Piacenza, Genoa, Bologna
A L P S
Nice, Monte Carlo, Côte d'Azur
MONACO
SAN MARINO
San Marino
Pisa, Florence, Perugia, Ancona
Cape Finisterre, A Coruña, Gijón, Santander, Bilbao, Bayonne, Vigo, León, Braga, Oporto, R. Douro
Cantabrian Mountains
Pyrenees
Aneto 3404
ANDORRA
Andorra la Vella
Toulouse, Montpellier, Avignon, Marseille, Perpignan
Costa Brava
Barcelona
Costa del Sol
PORTUGAL
Coimbra, Salamanca, Valladolid, Burgos, Pamplona, Zaragoza
R. Duero, R. Ebro
Madrid
SPAIN
Lisbon, Badajoz
R. Tagus
Sierra Morena
Córdoba, Seville
R. Guadalquivir
Granada
Sierra Nevada
Cape St Vincent, Faro, Cádiz
Albacete, Valencia, Alicante, Cartagena
Palma de Mallorca, Minorca, Majorca, Ibiza
Balearic Islands
Corsica, Ajaccio, Sardinia, Sassari, Cagliari
Tyrrhenian Sea
Rome
I T A L Y
Palermo, Sicily
Málaga, Almería
Gibraltar (UK)
Strait of Gibraltar
Tangier, Ceuta (Spain), Tétouan
Melilla (Spain)
Oran, Sidi Bel Abbès
MOROCCO
Rabat, Fez, Meknès, Casablanca, Marrakesh, Beni Mellal, Oujda
ALGERIA
Annaba, Bizerte, Tunis, Sousse, Tébessa, Gafsa, Sfax
TUNISIA
Gulf of Gabès

In this year...

- **1896** First modern Olympics are held in Athens.
- **2001** First European astronaut visits the International Space Station.
- **2008** Kosovo declares independence.

Albania H3 Capital : Tirana	Bosnia-Herzegovina H3 Capital : Sarajevo
Andorra E3 Capital : Andorra la Vella	Bulgaria I3 Capital : Sofia
Austria G4 Capital : Vienna	Croatia H4 Capital : Zagreb

Cyprus K1 Capital : Nicosia	Hungary H4 Capital : Budapest
France E4 Capital : Paris	Italy G3 Capital : Rome
Greece I2 Capital : Athens	Macedonia I3 Capital : Skopje

0 100 200 300 400 500 km

Scale : One centimetre on this map is the same as 100 kilometres on the ground.

Malta G2
Capital : Valletta

Portugal C2
Capital : Lisbon

Slovakia F4
Capital : Bratislava

Switzerland F4
Capital : Bern

Moldova J4
Capital : Chișinău

Romania I4
Capital : Bucharest

Slovenia G4
Capital : Ljubljana

Turkey J2
Capital : Ankara

Montenegro H3
Capital : Podgorica

Serbia I3
Capital : Belgrade

Spain C3
Capital : Madrid

Ukraine J4
Capital : Kiev

Largest country
Russian Federation 17 075 400 sq km

Country with most people
China 1 332 079 000

Russian Federation
Area 17 075 400 sq km
Population 142 836 000

Total population of Asia
(including Russian Federation)
4207 million

N
W E
S

ARCTIC OCEAN

EUROPE

St Petersburg

Yakutsk

Sea of
Okhotsk

Moscow

RUSSIAN FEDERATION

Sakhalin

1 ARMENIA
2 AZERBAIJAN
3 KYRGYZSTAN
4 TAJIKISTAN

Perm

Chelyabinsk

Omsk

Novosibirsk

Irkutsk

Lake
Baikal

Sapporo

Black
Sea

Volgograd

Ankara

GEORGIA

Astana

KAZAKHSTAN

Ulan
Bator

MONGOLIA

Harbin

Sea of
Japan
(East
Sea)

JAPAN

TURKEY

T'bilisi

Aral
Sea

Lake
Balkhash

Shenyang

NORTH
KOREA

Tokyo

CYPRUS

Yerevan

Baku

UZBEKISTAN

Pyongyang

Beijing

Kobe

Osaka

LEBANON
ISRAEL

SYRIA
Damascus

2

Caspian Sea

TURKMENISTAN

Tashkent

3

Bishkek

Ürümqi

Tianjin

SOUTH
KOREA

Seoul

Fukuoka

Amman
JORDAN

Baghdad

Ashgabat

4
Dushanbe

Lanzhou

Xi'an

Nanjing

Shanghai

IRAQ

Tehran

IRAN

Kabul

Islamabad

CHINA

Wuhan

Largest city
Tokyo 38 197 000

Kuwait

KUWAIT

AFGHANISTAN

Lahore

Chongqing

Riyadh

BAHRAIN
QATAR

UNITED
ARAB
EMIRATES

PAKISTAN

Delhi

New
Delhi

NEPAL

Kathmandu

Thimbu
BHUTAN

Guangzhou

Hong
Kong

T'aipei (Taibei)

TAIWAN

PACIFIC
OCEAN

SAUDI
ARABIA

Muscat

Karachi

BANGLADESH

Dhaka

Luzon

San'a

YEMEN

OMAN

INDIA

Kolkata

Mandalay

MYANMAR
(BURMA)

Hanoi

PHILIPPINES

Manila

Aden

Mumbai

Hyderabad

Nay Pyi Taw

Vientiane

Yangon

South
China
Sea

AFRICA

Socotra
(Yemen)

Arabian
Sea

Bay
of
Bengal

THAILAND

Bangkok

CAMBODIA

Mindanao

Davao

Chennai

Andaman Is
(India)

Phnom Penh

Ho Chi
Minh City

BRUNEI

Key to symbols

Countries

Capital city

Important city/town

SRI
LANKA

Nicobar Is
(India)

MALAYSIA

Sri Jayewardenepura Kotte

Colombo

Kuala Lumpur

MALDIVES

Putrajaya

Singapore

SINGAPORE

Borneo

Celebes

Makassar

Other maps showing regions of
Asia are on pages:
32-33 Russian Federation
34-35 Southwest and South Asia
36-37 East and Southeast Asia

32-33

34-35 36-37

INDIAN OCEAN

Sumatra

INDONESIA

Dili
EAST
TIMOR

Jakarta

Surabaya

Java

The British Isles
at the same scale

AUSTRALIA

Shanghai is China's largest city.

A fruit stall in the Chinatown market place,
Kuala Lumpur, Malaysia.

0 500 1000 1500 2000 2500 km

Scale : One centimetre on this map is the same as 500 kilometres on the ground.

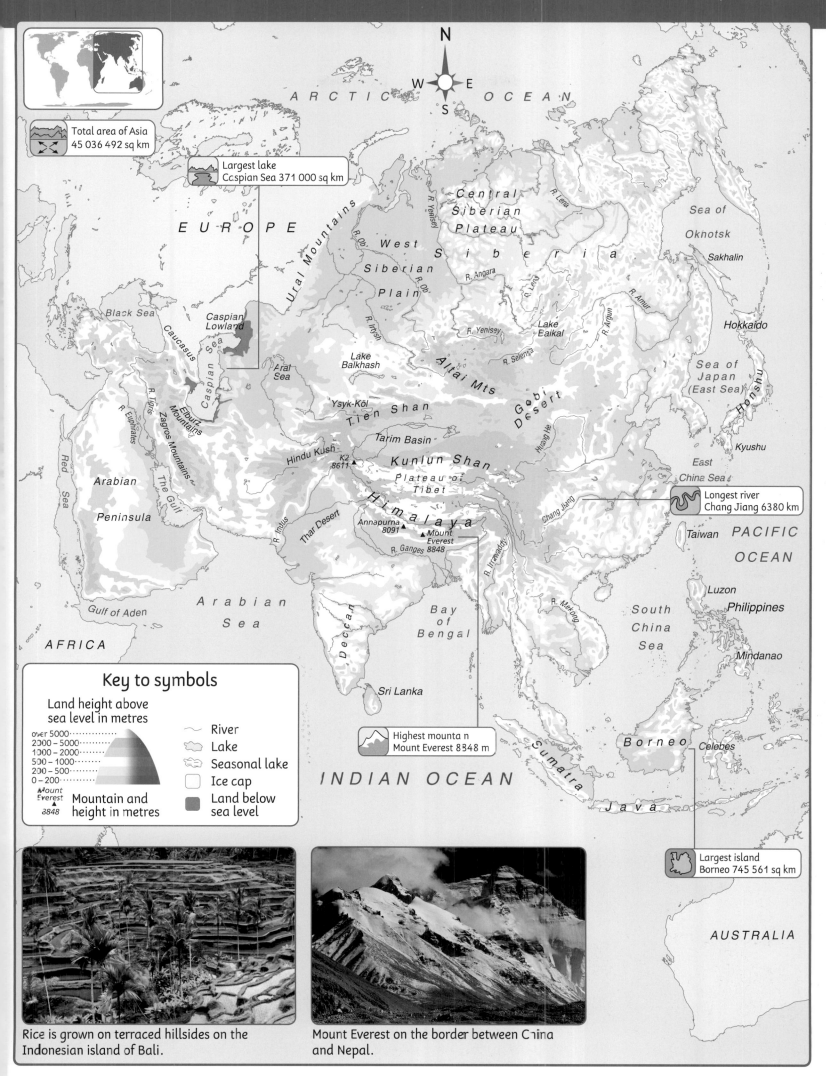

Total area of Asia
45 036 492 sq km

Largest lake
Caspian Sea 371 000 sq km

ARCTIC OCEAN

N
W E
S

EUROPE

Black Sea

Caucasus

R. Tigris

R. Euphrates

Zagros Mountains

Elburz Mountains

Caspian Sea

Caspian Lowland

Ural Mountains

R. Ob

West Siberian Plain

Aral Sea

R. Irtysh

R. Ob

Lake Balkhash

R. Yenisey

Central Siberian Plateau

R. Lena

Siberia

R. Angara

R. Lena

Lake Baikal

R. Selenga

R. Yenisey

R. Amur

R. Argun

Sea of Okhotsk

Sakhalin

Hokkaido

Sea of Japan (East Sea)

Honshu

Ysyk-Köl

Tien Shan

Altai Mts

Gobi Desert

Kyushu

Hindu Kush

K2 8611

Tarim Basin

Kunlun Shan

Huang He

East China Sea

Longest river
Chang Jiang 6380 km

Arabian Peninsula

The Gulf

R. Indus

Thar Desert

Plateau of Tibet

Himalaya

Annapurna 8091

Mount Everest 8848

R. Ganges

Chang Jiang

R. Irrawaddy

PACIFIC OCEAN

Taiwan

Red Sea

Gulf of Aden

AFRICA

Arabian Sea

Deccan

Bay of Bengal

R. Mekong

Luzon

Philippines

South China Sea

Mindanao

Sri Lanka

Highest mountain
Mount Everest 8848 m

INDIAN OCEAN

Sumatra

Borneo

Celebes

Largest island
Borneo 745 561 sq km

Java

AUSTRALIA

Key to symbols

Land height above sea level in metres

over 5000
2000 – 5000
1000 – 2000
500 – 1000
200 – 500
0 – 200

Mount Everest 3848

Mountain and height in metres

~ River

Lake

Seasonal lake

Ice cap

Land below sea level

Rice is grown on terraced hillsides on the Indonesian island of Bali.

Mount Everest on the border between China and Nepal.

0 500 1000 1500 2000 2500 km

Scale : One centimetre on this map is the same as 500 kilometres on the ground.

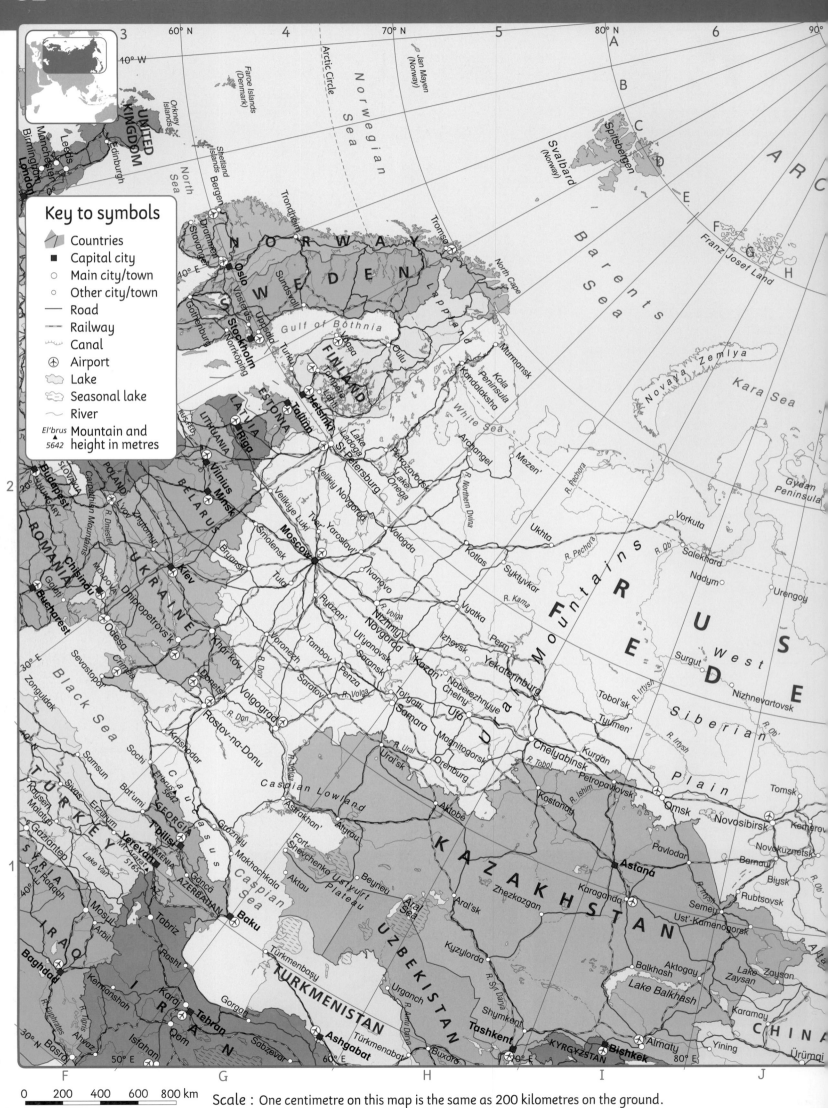

Key to symbols

- Countries
- ■ Capital city
- ○ Main city/town
- ○ Other city/town
- — Road
- Railway
- Canal
- ✈ Airport
- Lake
- Seasonal lake
- River
- El'brus ▲ Mountain and
- 5642 height in metres

Scale : One centimetre on this map is the same as 200 kilometres on the ground.

0 200 400 600 800 km

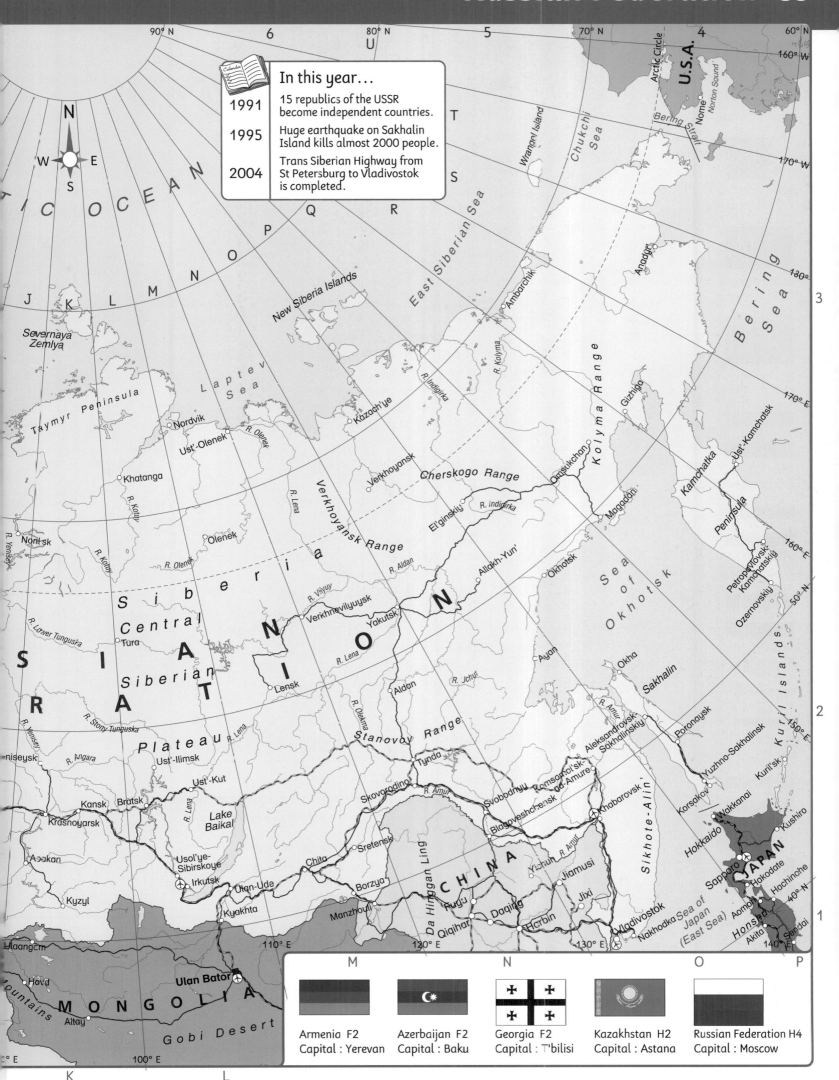

In this year...

1991 — 15 republics of the USSR become independent countries.

1995 — Huge earthquake on Sakhalin Island kills almost 2000 people.

2004 — Trans Siberian Highway from St Petersburg to Vladivostok is completed.

ARCTIC OCEAN

U.S.A.

Arctic Circle

Nome

Norton Sound

Bering Strait

Chukchi Sea

Wrangel Island

East Siberian Sea

Amborchik

Anadyr

New Siberia Islands

Laptev Sea

Severnaya Zemlya

Taymyr Peninsula

Nordvik

R. Olenek

Ust'-Olenek

Kazach'ye

R. Kolyma

R. Indigirka

Bering Sea

Khatanga

Verkhoyansk

Cherskogo Range

Omsukchan

Kolyma Range

Gizhiga

Ust'-Kamchatsk

R. Kotuy

R. Olenek

R. Lena

Verkhoyansk Range

El'ginskiy

R. Indigirka

Magadan

Kamchatka

Peninsula

Noril'sk

R. Yenisey

Olenek

R. Olenek

R. Aldan

Allakh-Yun'

Okhotsk

Petropavlovsk-Kamchatskiy

R. Lower Tunguska

Tura

R. Vilyuy

Verkhnevilyuysk

Yakutsk

Sea of Okhotsk

Ozernovskiy

S I B E R I A N

F E D E R A T I O N

R U S S I A N

Central

R. Lena

Ayan

Okha

Siberian

Lensk

Aldan

R. Uchur

Sakhalin

Plateau

R. Lena

R. Olekma

Stanovoy Range

R. Amur

Aleksandrovsk-Sakhalinskiy

Poronaysk

Yuzhno-Sakhalinsk

R. Stony Tunguska

Tynda

Kuril Islands

niseysk

Ust'-Ilimsk

Komsomol'sk-nad-Amure

Kuril'sk

R. Yenisey

R. Angara

Ust'-Kut

Skovorodino

R. Amur

Svobodnyy

Khabarovsk

Korsakov

Wakkanai

Krasnoyarsk

Kansk

Bratsk

R. Lena

Lake Baikal

Sretensk

Blagoveshchensk

Sikhote-Alin'

Hokkaido

Kushiro

Abakan

Chita

Da Hinggan Ling

CHINA

Yichun

R. Amur

Jiamusi

Sapporo

JAPAN

Hakodate

Usol'ye-Sibirskoye

Irkutsk

Borzya

Fugu

Jixi

Vladivostok

Nakhodka

Aomori

Hachinohe

Kyzyl

Ulan-Ude

Manzhouli

Daqing

Harbin

Sea of Japan (East Sea)

Honshu

Akita

Sendai

Kyakhta

Qiqihar

laangom

Hovd

Ulan Bator

MONGOLIA

Altay

Gobi Desert

Mountains

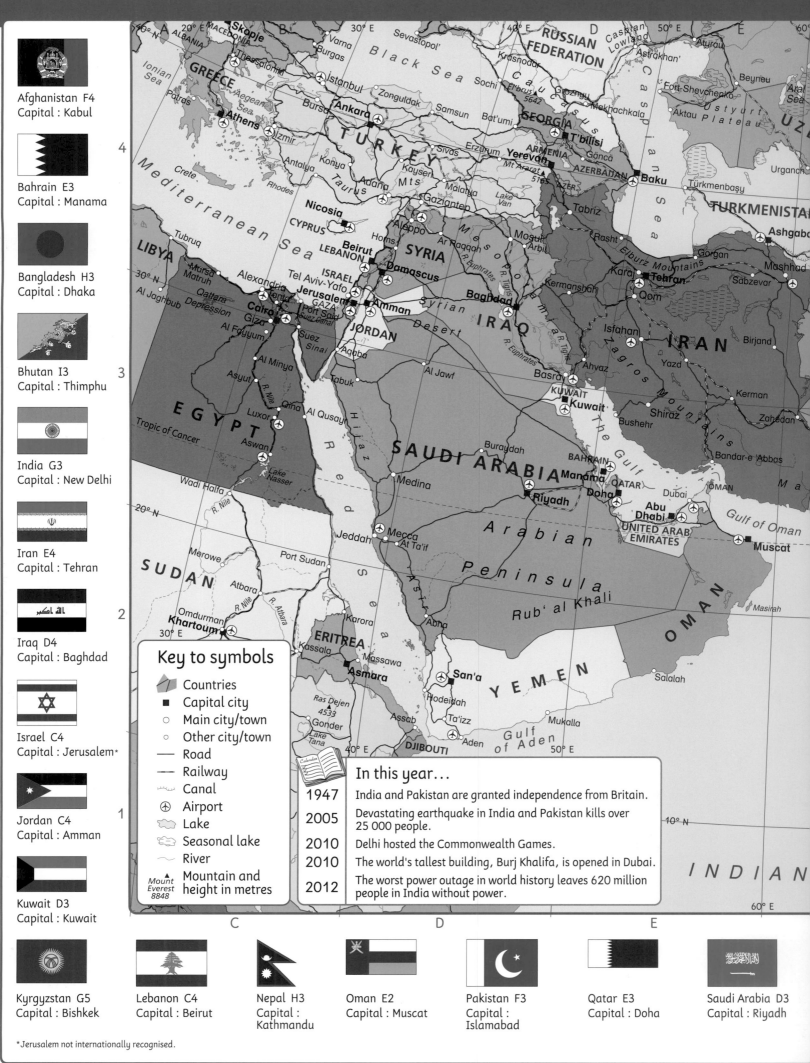

Afghanistan F4
Capital : Kabul

Bahrain E3
Capital : Manama

Bangladesh H3
Capital : Dhaka

Bhutan I3
Capital : Thimphu

India G3
Capital : New Delhi

Iran E4
Capital : Tehran

Iraq D4
Capital : Baghdad

Israel C4
Capital : Jerusalem*

Jordan C4
Capital : Amman

Kuwait D3
Capital : Kuwait

Kyrgyzstan G5
Capital : Bishkek

Lebanon C4
Capital : Beirut

Nepal H3
Capital : Kathmandu

Oman E2
Capital : Muscat

Pakistan F3
Capital : Islamabad

Qatar E3
Capital : Doha

Saudi Arabia D3
Capital : Riyadh

*Jerusalem not internationally recognised.

Key to symbols

- Countries
- ■ Capital city
- ○ Main city/town
- ○ Other city/town
- — Road
- ┼ Railway
- ∿ Canal
- ⊕ Airport
- Lake
- Seasonal lake
- ～ River
- ▲ Mountain and height in metres
  Mount Everest 8848

In this year...

1947	India and Pakistan are granted independence from Britain.
2005	Devastating earthquake in India and Pakistan kills over 25 000 people.
2010	Delhi hosted the Commonwealth Games.
2010	The world's tallest building, Burj Khalifa, is opened in Dubai.
2012	The worst power outage in world history leaves 620 million people in India without power.

0 200 400 600 800 km

Scale : One centimetre on this map is the same as 200 kilometres on the ground.

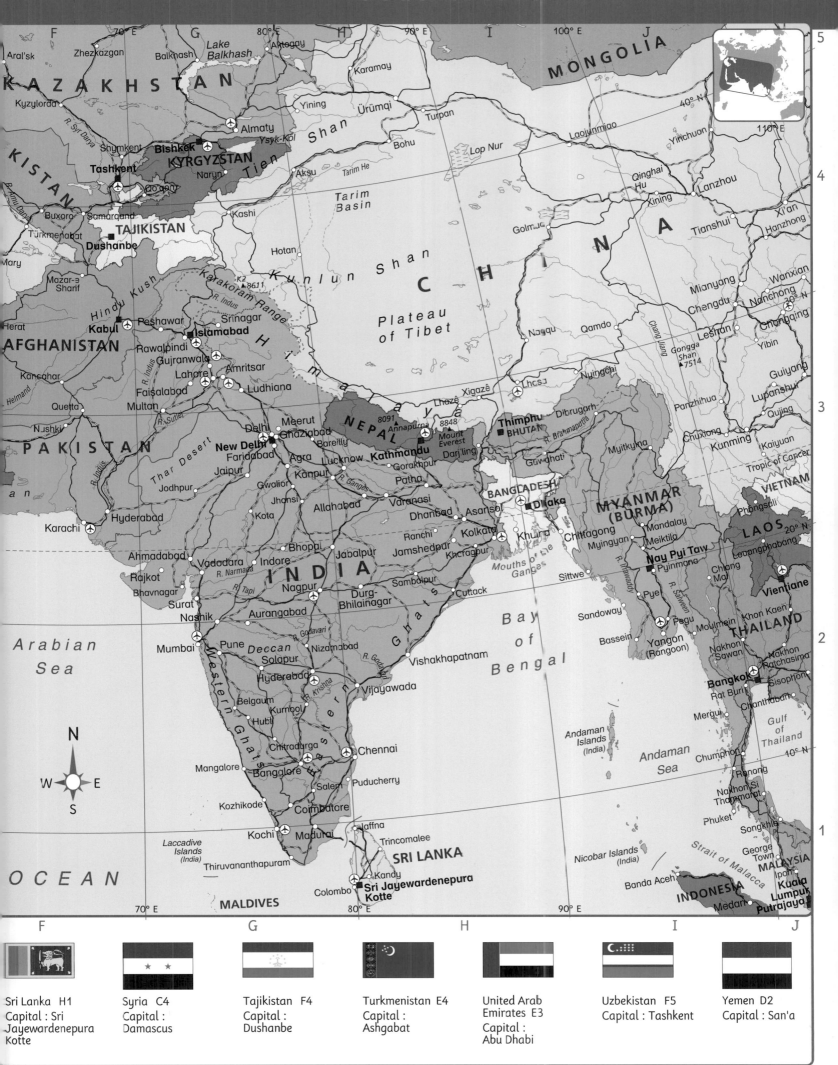

F   G   H   I   J

Sri Lanka H1
Capital : Sri Jayewardenepura Kotte

Syria C4
Capital : Damascus

Tajikistan F4
Capital : Dushanbe

Turkmenistan E4
Capital : Ashgabat

United Arab Emirates E3
Capital : Abu Dhabi

Uzbekistan F5
Capital : Tashkent

Yemen D2
Capital : San'a

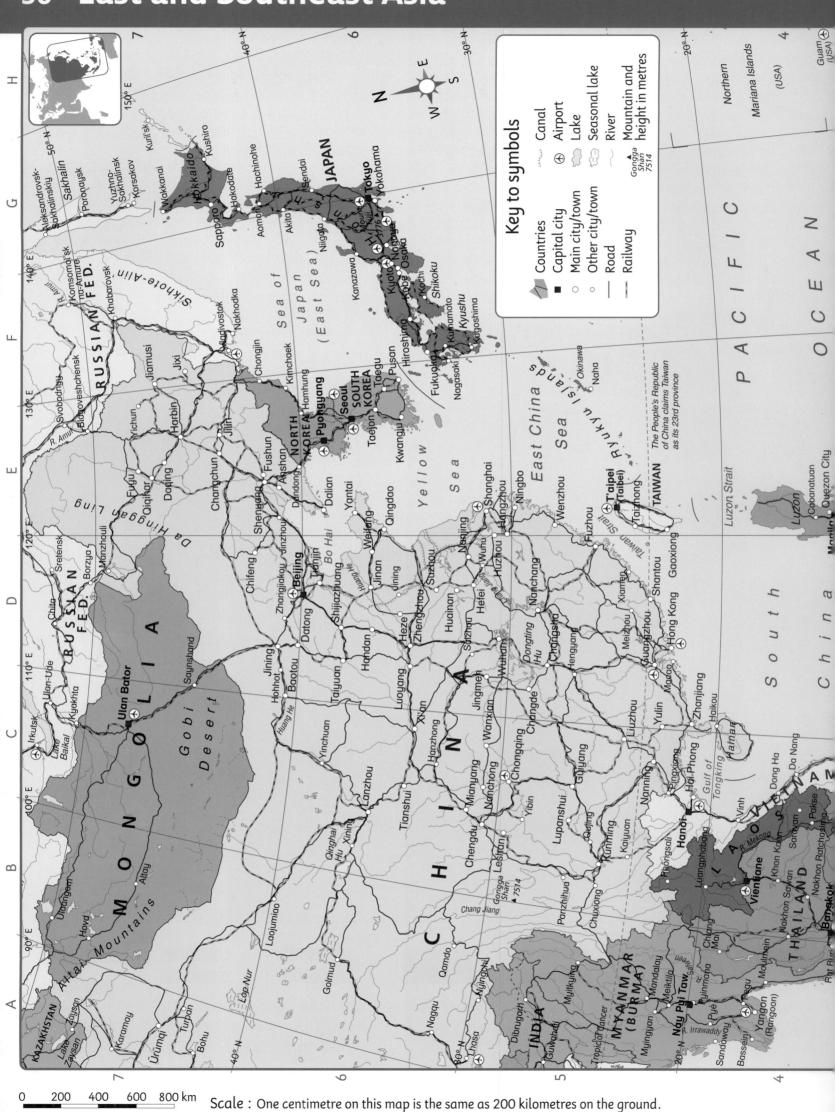

Key to symbols

Countries	Canal	Airport ⊕
Capital city ■	Road	Lake
Main city/town ○	Railway	Seasonal lake
Other city/town ○		River
		Mountain and height in metres
		▲ Gongga Shan 7514

Scale : One centimetre on this map is the same as 200 kilometres on the ground.

0   200   400   600   800 km

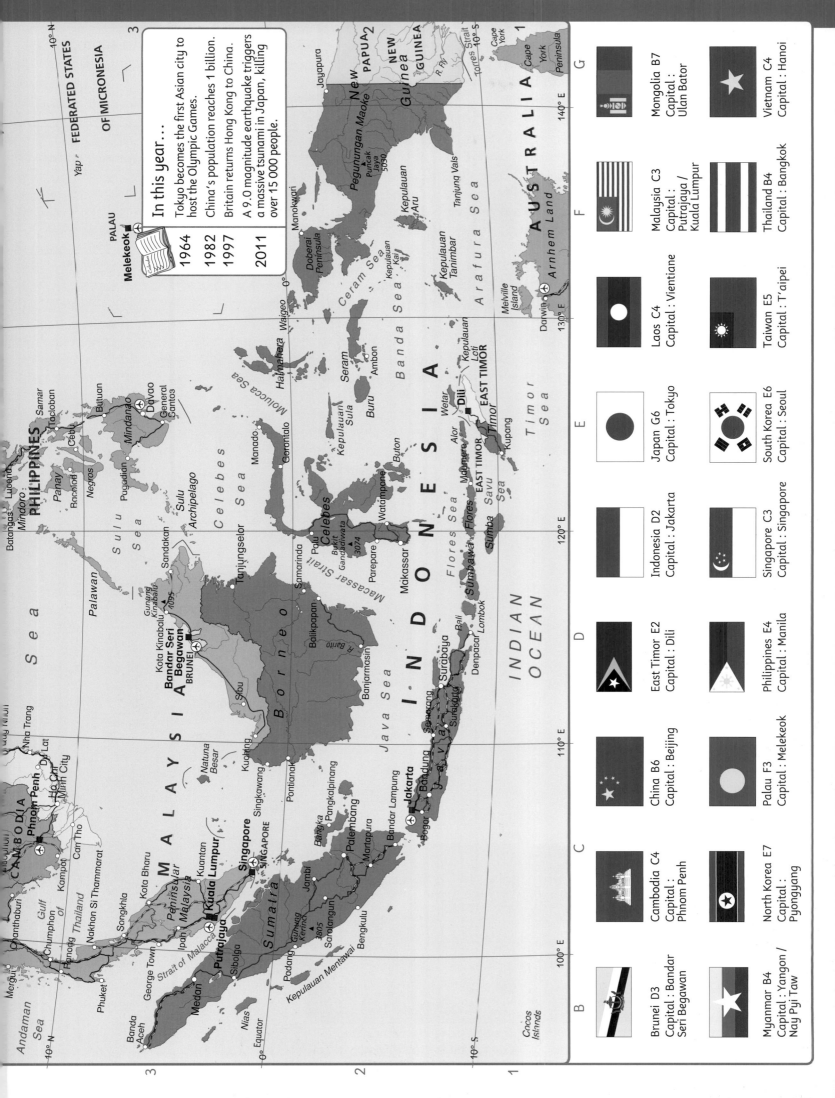

In this year...

1964	Tokyo becomes the first Asian city to host the Olympic Games.
1982	China's population reaches 1 billion.
1997	Britain returns Hong Kong to China.
2011	A 9.0 magnitude earthquake triggers a massive tsunami in Japan, killing over 15 000 people.

Brunei D3
Capital: Bandar Seri Begawan

Myanmar B4
Capital: Yangon / Nay Pyi Taw

Cambodia C4
Capital: Phnom Penh

North Korea E7
Capital: Pyongyang

China B6
Capital: Beijing

Palau F3
Capital: Melekeok

East Timor E2
Capital: Dili

Philippines E4
Capital: Manila

Indonesia D2
Capital: Jakarta

Singapore C3
Capital: Singapore

Japan G6
Capital: Tokyo

South Korea E6
Capital: Seoul

Laos C4
Capital: Vientiane

Taiwan E5
Capital: T'aipei

Malaysia C3
Capital: Putrajaya / Kuala Lumpur

Thailand B4
Capital: Bangkok

Mongolia B7
Capital: Ulan Bator

Vietnam C4
Capital: Hanoi

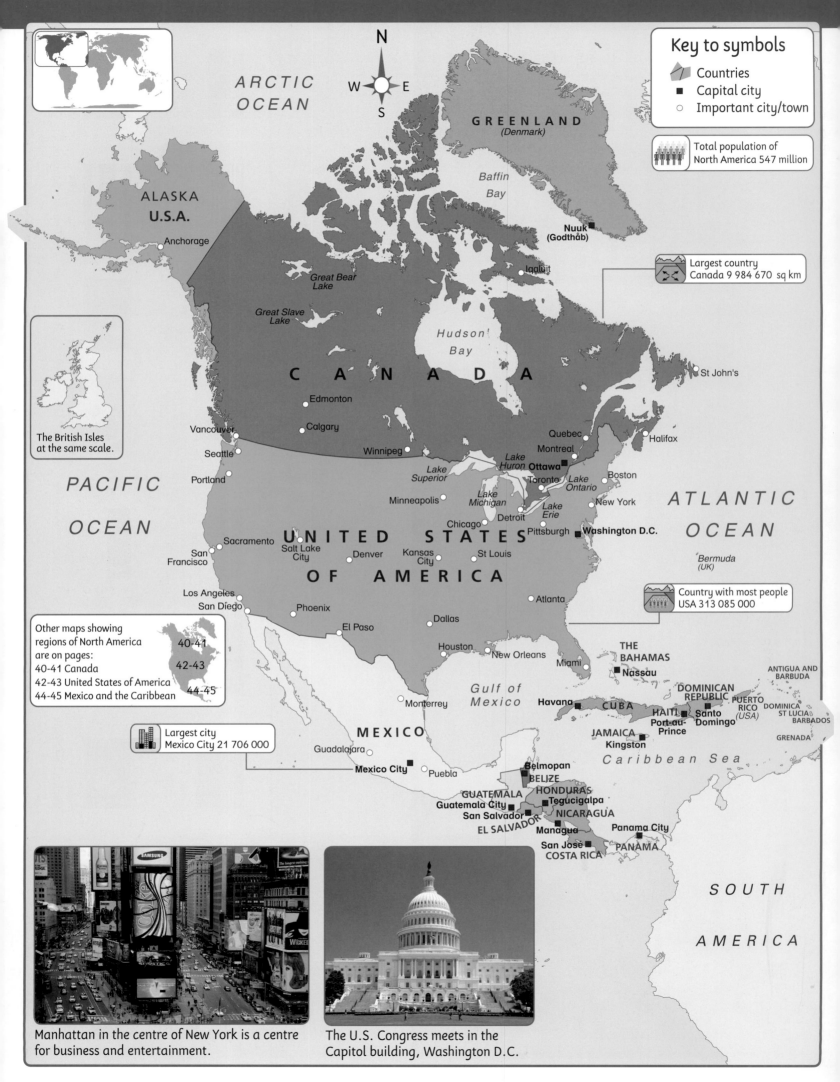

ARCTIC OCEAN

GREENLAND
(Denmark)

Baffin Bay

ALASKA
U.S.A.

Anchorage

Key to symbols

Countries
■ Capital city
○ Important city/town

Total population of
North America 547 million

Nuuk
(Godthåb)

Iqaluit

Largest country
Canada 9 984 670 sq km

Great Bear Lake

Great Slave Lake

Hudson Bay

C A N A D A

St John's

Edmonton

The British Isles at the same scale.

Calgary

Vancouver

Quebec

Halifax

Seattle

Winnipeg

Montreal

Lake Huron

Ottawa

PACIFIC OCEAN

Portland

Lake Superior

Toronto

Lake Ontario

Boston

Minneapolis

Lake Michigan

Detroit

Lake Erie

New York

ATLANTIC OCEAN

Chicago

Sacramento

U N I T E D   S T A T E S

Pittsburgh

Washington D.C.

San Francisco

Salt Lake City

Denver

Kansas City

St Louis

Bermuda (UK)

O F   A M E R I C A

Country with most people
USA 313 085 000

Los Angeles

Phoenix

Atlanta

San Diego

El Paso

Dallas

Other maps showing regions of North America are on pages:
40-41 Canada
42-43 United States of America
44-45 Mexico and the Caribbean

40-41

42-43

44-45

Houston

New Orleans

Miami

THE BAHAMAS

Nassau

ANTIGUA AND BARBUDA

Gulf of Mexico

Monterrey

Havana

DOMINICAN REPUBLIC

PUERTO RICO (USA)

CUBA

HAITI

Santo Domingo

DOMINICA

ST LUCIA

Largest city
Mexico City 21 706 000

M E X I C O

Port-au-Prince

BARBADOS

JAMAICA

Kingston

Caribbean Sea

GRENADA

Guadalajara

Mexico City

Puebla

Belmopan

BELIZE

GUATEMALA

HONDURAS

Guatemala City

Tegucigalpa

San Salvador

NICARAGUA

EL SALVADOR

Managua

Panama City

San José

PANAMA

COSTA RICA

SOUTH

AMERICA

Manhattan in the centre of New York is a centre for business and entertainment.

The U.S. Congress meets in the Capitol building, Washington D.C.

0   400   800   1200   1600   2000 km

Scale : One centimetre on this map is the same as 400 kilometres on the ground.

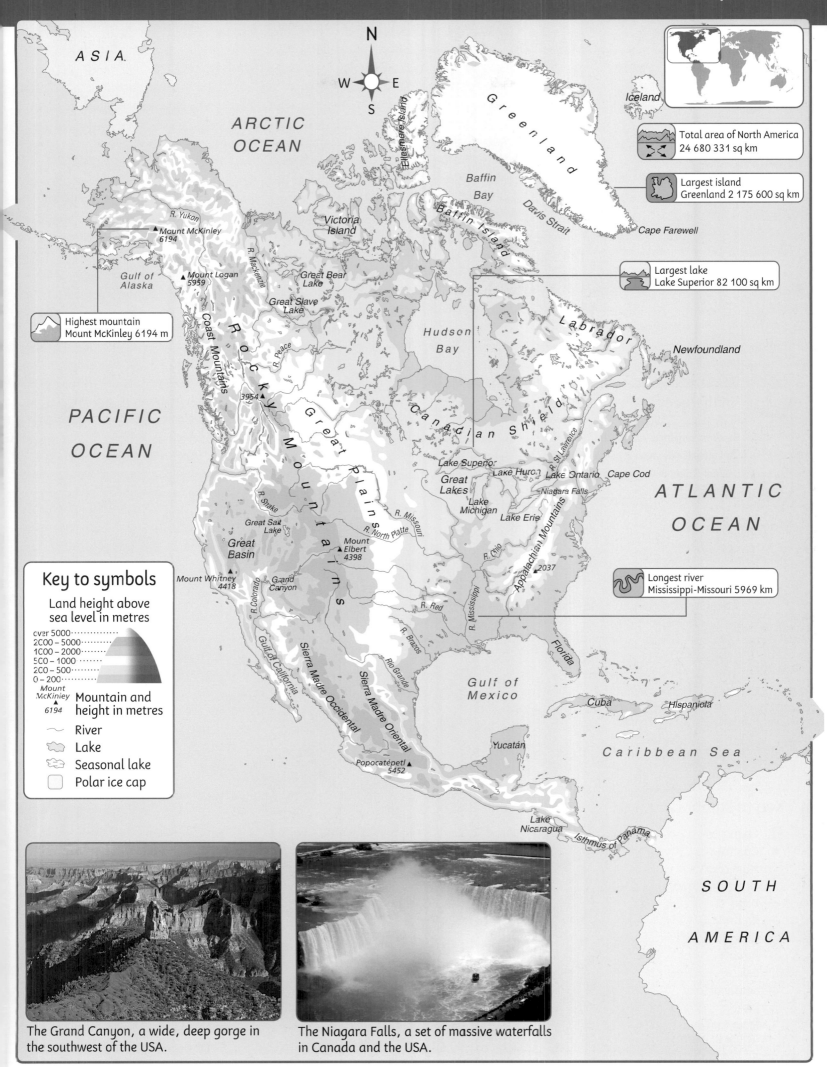

ASIA

ARCTIC OCEAN

Iceland

Greenland

N
W E
S

Elsmere Island

Baffin Bay

Baffin Island

Davis Strait

Cape Farewell

Total area of North America
24 680 331 sq km

Largest island
Greenland 2 175 600 sq km

R. Yukon

Mount McKinley 6194

Gulf of Alaska

Mount Logan 5959

Victoria Island

Great Bear Lake

Great Slave Lake

R. Mackenzie

Hudson Bay

Labrador

Newfoundland

Largest lake
Lake Superior 82 100 sq km

Highest mountain
Mount McKinley 6194 m

Coast Mountains

Rocky Mountains

R. Peace

3954

Canadian Shield

R. St Lawrence

PACIFIC OCEAN

Great Plains

Lake Superior

Great Lakes

Lake Huron

Lake Ontario

Cape Cod

ATLANTIC OCEAN

Appalachian Mountains

R. Snake

Lake Michigan

Lake Erie

Niagara Falls

Great Salt Lake

Mount Elbert 4398

R. North Platte

R. Missouri

R. Ohio

2037

Great Basin

Grand Canyon

R. Colorado

Mount Whitney 4418

R. Mississippi

R. Red

Longest river
Mississippi-Missouri 5969 km

Gulf of California

Sierra Madre Occidental

Sierra Madre Oriental

R. Brazos

Rio Grande

Florida

Gulf of Mexico

Cuba

Hispaniola

Caribbean Sea

Yucatán

Popocatépetl 5452

Lake Nicaragua

Isthmus of Panama

SOUTH AMERICA

Key to symbols

Land height above sea level in metres

over 5000
2000 – 5000
1000 – 2000
500 – 1000
200 – 500
0 – 200

Mount McKinley 6194 ▲ Mountain and height in metres

⌒ River

◯ Lake

◯ Seasonal lake

▢ Polar ice cap

The Grand Canyon, a wide, deep gorge in the southwest of the USA.

The Niagara Falls, a set of massive waterfalls in Canada and the USA.

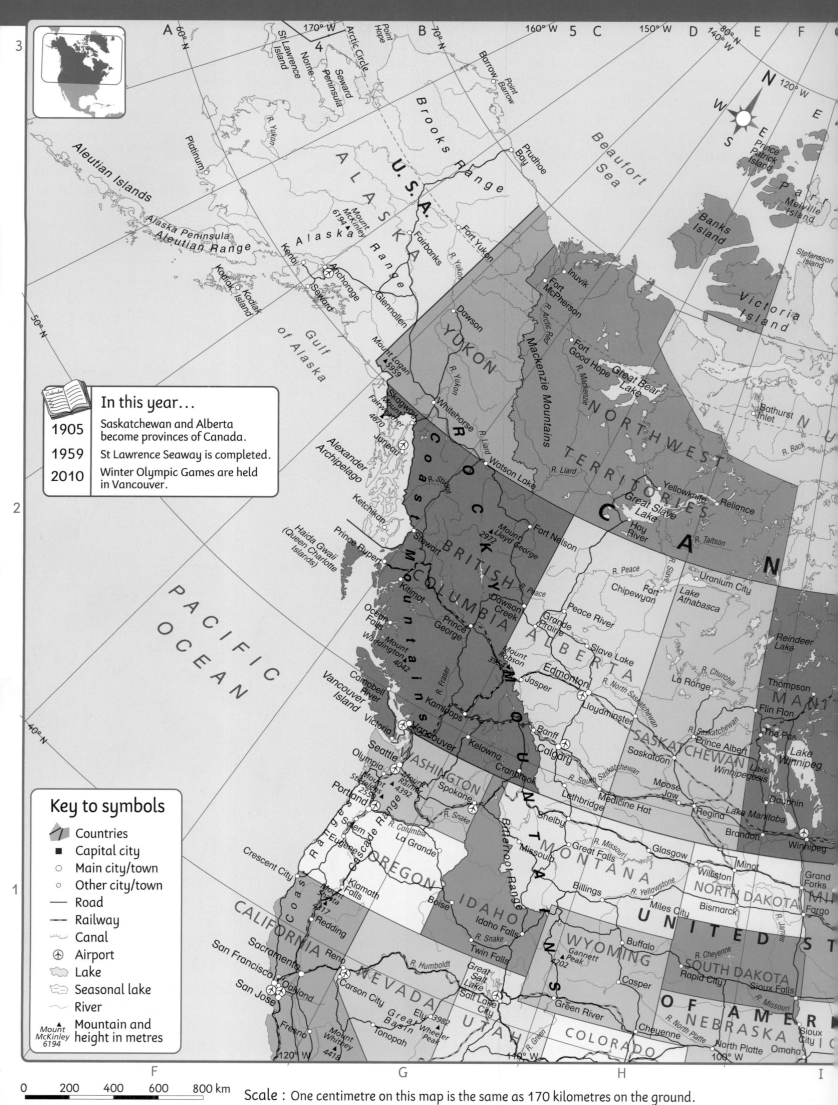

In this year...

1905 Saskatchewan and Alberta become provinces of Canada.

1959 St Lawrence Seaway is completed.

2010 Winter Olympic Games are held in Vancouver.

Key to symbols

- Countries
- ■ Capital city
- ○ Main city/town
- ○ Other city/town
- ─── Road
- ─── Railway
- Canal
- ⊕ Airport
- Lake
- Seasonal lake
- River
- ▲ Mount McKinley 6194 Mountain and height in metres

Scale : One centimetre on this map is the same as 170 kilometres on the ground.

0 200 400 600 800 km

H   I   J   K   L   M   N   O   P   S   Q   4
6

Queen
100°W
Elizabeth
80°W   40°W   80°N   O   30°W   40°N   30°W   70°N   Q   60°N   60°N   90°N
Ellef
Ringnes
Island
Islands
burst
Island
Devon Island
Resolute
Somerset
Island
Arctic Bay
Baffin Bay
GREENLAND (Denmark)
Arctic Circle
Seyðisfjörður   Höfn
ICELAND
Reykjavik
Kong Christian IX Land
Gunnbjorn Field 3700
Isafjörður
Denmark Strait

Prince of Wales Island
Gulf of Boothia
Boothia Peninsula
Cape Parry
Thule
Baffin Island
Clyde River
Saqqaq
Disko I.
Tasiilaq
Kong Frederick VI Kyst

King William Island
Melville Peninsula
Prince Charles Island
Pangnirtung
Nuuk (Godthåb)
Davis Strait
Cape Farewell

Repulse Bay
Foxe Basin
Amadjuak Lake
Iqaluit
Nanortalik

NUNAVUT
Southampton Island
Coral Harbour
Hudson Strait
Labrador Sea

Qamanittuaq
Coats Island
Mansel Island
Salluit
Kangiqsujuaq
NEWFOUNDLAND AND LABRADOR

Rankin Inlet
CANADA
Inukjuak
Kangiqsualujjuaq
R. George
Hopedale

Churchill
Hudson Bay
Kuujjuaq
Schefferville
Smallwood Reservoir
Happy Valley-Goose Bay
Port Hope Simpson
St Anthony

Nelson
Belcher Islands
Caniapiscau
Labrador
R. Churchill
Labrador City

MANITOBA
Fort Severn
Reservoir La Grande 2
Chisasibi
Reservoir La Grande 3
R. Eastmain
QUEBEC
Havre-St-Pierre
Grand Falls-Windsor
Newfoundland
St John's

Sandy Lake
R. Albany
Fort Albany
Eastmain
Lac Mistassini
Sept-Îles
Baie-Comeau
Gulf of St Lawrence
Channel-Port aux-Basques
St Pierre and Miquelon (France)

ONTARIO
Moosonee
R. Moose
R. Harricana
Chibougamau
Chicoutimi
R. St Lawrence
Bathurst
NEW BRUNSWICK
Charlottetown
P.E.I.
Sydney
Cape Breton Island

Sioux Lookout
Timmins
Jonquière
Rivière-du-Loup
Moncton
NOVA SCOTIA

Fort Frances
Lake Nipigon
Longlac
Nipigon
Val-d'Or
Québec
Saint John
Halifax

Kenora
Thunder Bay
Chapleau
Trois-Rivières
Montréal
Sherbrooke
Mount Washington 1918
MAINE
Augusta
Cape Sable
Yarmouth

MINNESOTA
Lake Superior
Sault Sainte Marie
Sudbury
North Bay
R. Ottawa
Ottawa
Kingston
VER.
N.H.
Portland
Cape Cod

St Paul
Duluth
Escanaba
Lake Michigan
MICHIGAN
Toronto
Oshawa
Lake Ontario
Rochester
MASS.
Boston
Providence

Albert Lea
Minneapolis
Green Bay
WISCONSIN
Flint
Hamilton
Buffalo
NEW YORK
Albany
Hartford
Long Island

Milwaukee
Detroit
Lake Erie
Erie
Cleveland
Allentown
New York

Cedar Rapids
Chicago
South Bend
Toledo
PENN.
90°W
80°W
70°W
60°W
Des Moines

J   K   L   M

ATLANTIC OCEAN

50°N
2
40°N
1

Greenland N5
Capital : Nuuk

Canada G4
Capital : Ottawa

CO.   CONNECTICUT
MASS.   MASSACHUSETTS
N.H.   NEW HAMPSHIRE
P.E.I.   PRINCE EDWARD ISLAND
PENN.   PENNSYLVANIA
R.I.   RHODE ISLAND
VER.   VERMONT

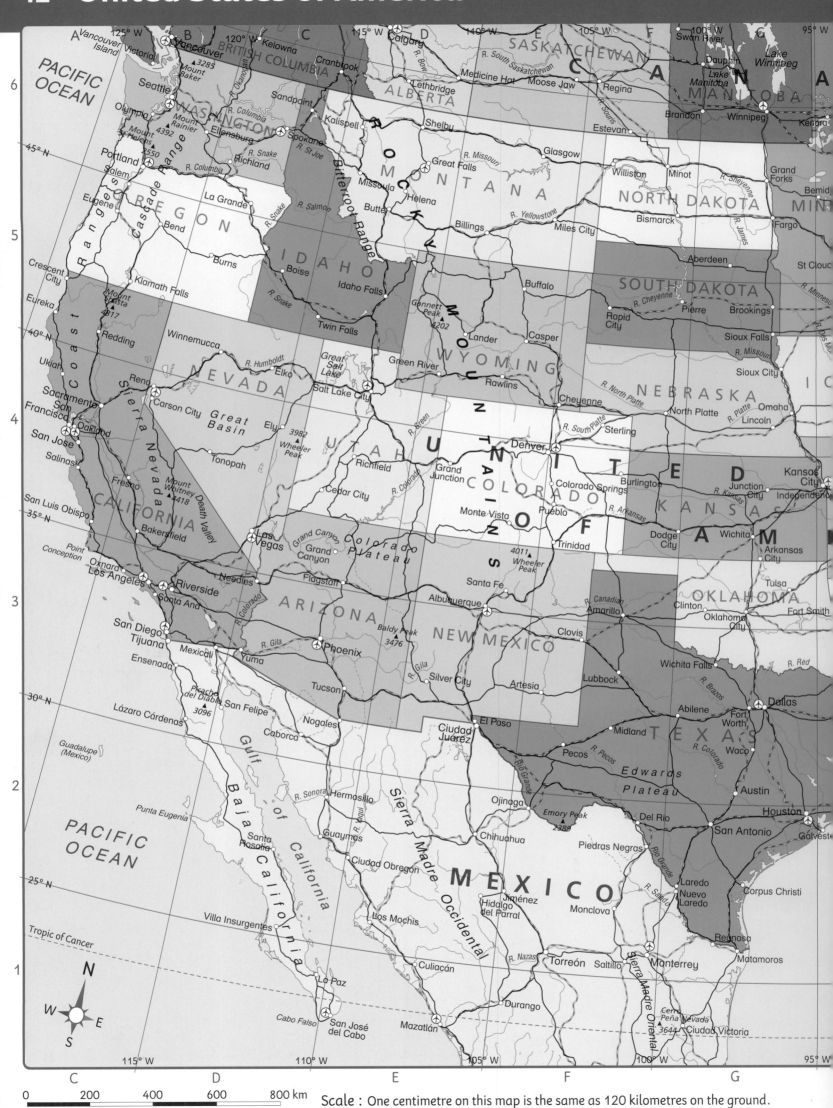

Scale : One centimetre on this map is the same as 120 kilometres on the ground.

0   200   400   600   800 km

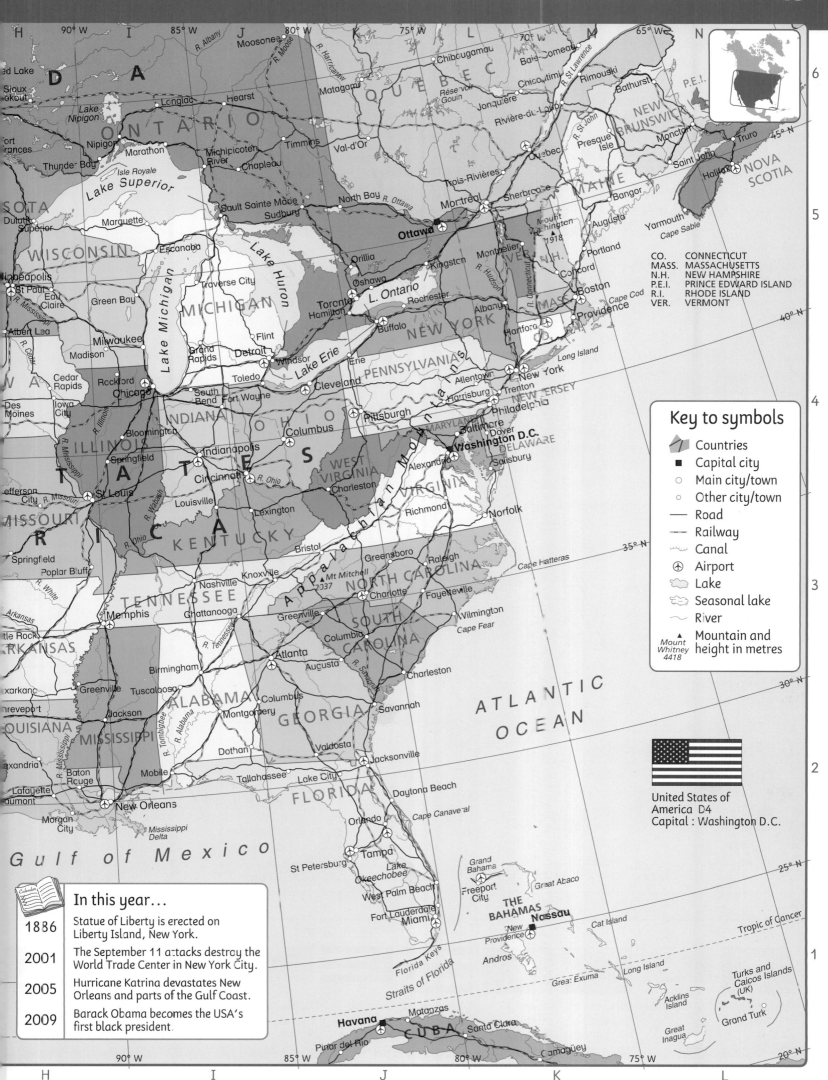

Key to symbols

🔺 Countries
■ Capital city
○ Main city/town
○ Other city/town
── Road
── Railway
⌇⌇ Canal
⊕ Airport
◠ Lake
◡ Seasonal lake
⌇ River
▲ Mountain and
Mount height in metres
Whitney
4418

CO.   CONNECTICUT
MASS. MASSACHUSETTS
N.H.   NEW HAMPSHIRE
P.E.I.   PRINCE EDWARD ISLAND
R.I.   RHODE ISLAND
VER.   VERMONT

United States of
America D4
Capital : Washington D.C.

In this year...

1886   Statue of Liberty is erected on Liberty Island, New York.

2001   The September 11 attacks destroy the World Trade Center in New York City.

2005   Hurricane Katrina devastates New Orleans and parts of the Gulf Coast.

2009   Barack Obama becomes the USA's first black president.

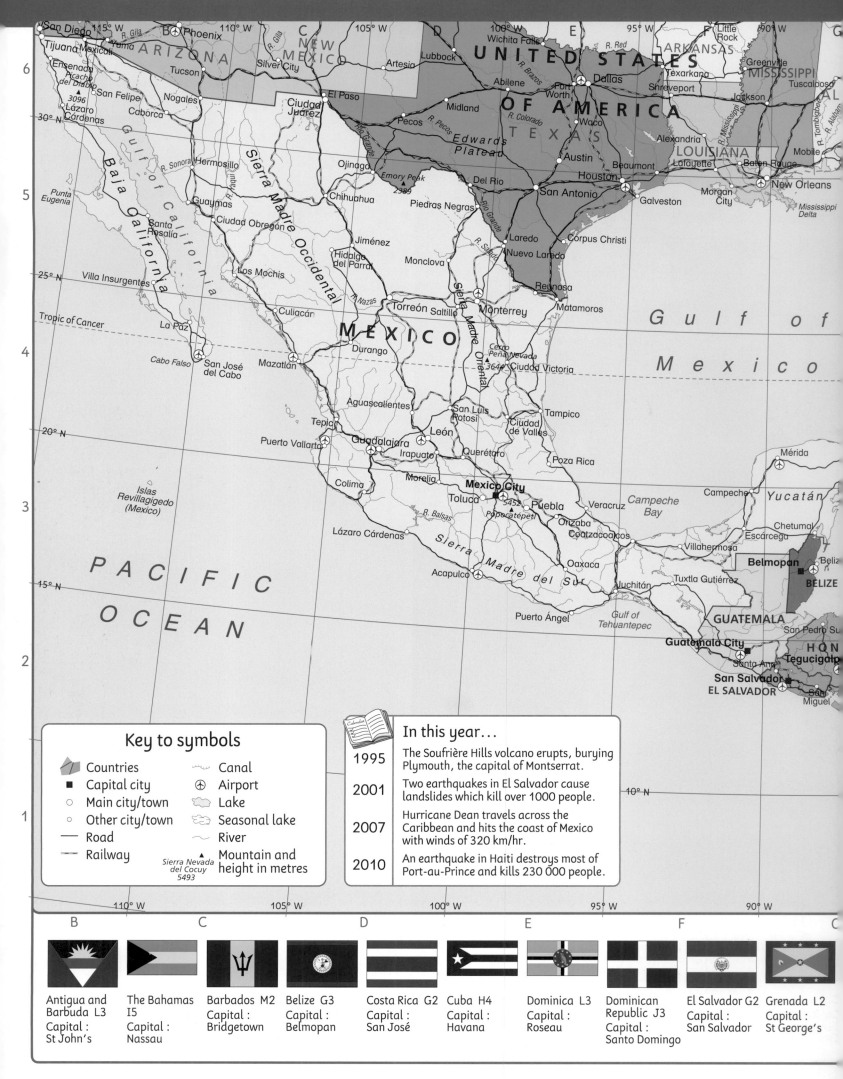

Key to symbols

- ◣ Countries
- ■ Capital city
- ○ Main city/town
- ○ Other city/town
- — Road
- ⊷ Railway
- ⌒ Canal
- ⊕ Airport
- ◇ Lake
- ⌣ Seasonal lake
- ~ River
- ▲ Mountain and height in metres

Sierra Nevada del Cocuy 5493

In this year...

1995	The Soufrière Hills volcano erupts, burying Plymouth, the capital of Montserrat.
2001	Two earthquakes in El Salvador cause landslides which kill over 1000 people.
2007	Hurricane Dean travels across the Caribbean and hits the coast of Mexico with winds of 320 km/hr.
2010	An earthquake in Haiti destroys most of Port-au-Prince and kills 230 000 people.

Antigua and Barbuda L3
Capital : St John's

The Bahamas I5
Capital : Nassau

Barbados M2
Capital : Bridgetown

Belize G3
Capital : Belmopan

Costa Rica G2
Capital : San José

Cuba H4
Capital : Havana

Dominica L3
Capital : Roseau

Dominican Republic J3
Capital : Santo Domingo

El Salvador G2
Capital : San Salvador

Grenada L2
Capital : St George's

Scale : One centimetre on this map is the same as 135 kilometres on the ground.

0   200   400   600   800 km

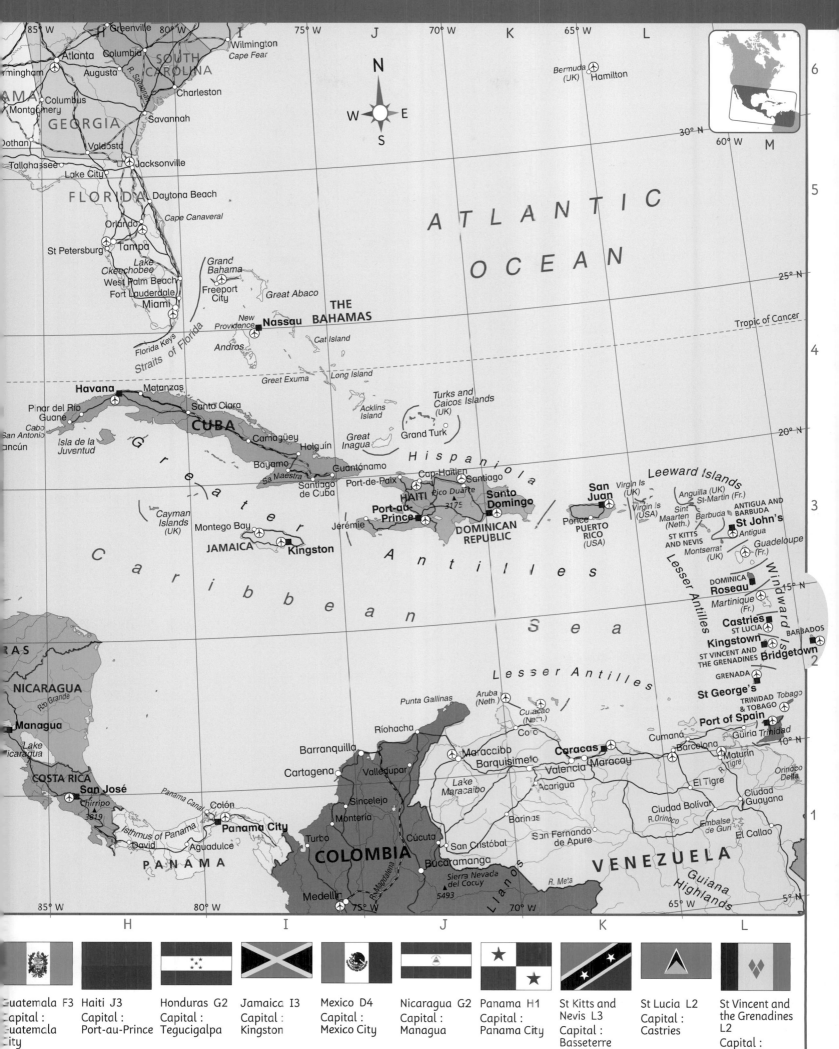

85° W   80° W   I   75° W   J   70° W   K   65° W   L

6

Greenville
Atlanta Columbia   SOUTH   Wilmington
Birmingham Augusta   CAROLINA   Cape Fear
Columbus Montgomery   N   Bermuda (UK) Hamilton
GEORGIA   W   E   60° W   M
Dothan   Savannah   S   30° N
Tallahassee   Valdosta

5

Lake City   Jacksonville
FLORIDA   Daytona Beach   A T L A N T I C
Orlando   Cape Canaveral
St Petersburg Tampa   O C E A N   25° N
Lake Okeechobee   Grand Bahama
West Palm Beach   Freeport City   Great Abaco
Fort Lauderdale   THE
Miami   New Providence Nassau BAHAMAS   Tropic of Cancer

4

Florida Keys Straits of Florida   Andros Cat Island
Great Exuma   Long Island
Havana   Matanzas   Acklins Island   Turks and Caicos Islands (UK)
Pinar del Río Guane   Santa Clara   CUBA   Great Inagua Grand Turk   20° N
Cabo San Antonio   Isla de la Juventud   Camagüey Holguín   Hispaniola   Leeward Islands
Cancún   Bayamo   Guantánamo   Cap-Haïtien Santiago   Virgin Is (UK)   Anguilla (UK) St-Martin (Fr.)
    Sa Maestra   Santiago de Cuba Port-de-Paix   HAITI Pico Duarte 3175 Santo Domingo San Juan Virgin Is (USA)   Sint Maarten (Neth.) Barbuda   ANTIGUA AND BARBUDA

3

Greater   Cayman Islands (UK)   Montego Bay   Port-au-Prince Jérémie   DOMINICAN REPUBLIC Ponce PUERTO RICO (USA)   ST KITTS AND NEVIS Montserrat (UK)   St John's Antigua Guadeloupe (Fr.)
JAMAICA Kingston   Antilles   DOMINICA Roseau   Windward Is
C a r i b b e a n   Martinique (Fr.)   15° N
    Castries ST LUCIA   BARBADOS

2

    Lesser Antilles   S e a   Kingstown ST VINCENT AND THE GRENADINES Bridgetown
NICARAGUA   Lesser Antilles   GRENADA
Managua   Punta Gallinas   Aruba (Neth) Curaçao (Neth.)   St George's   TRINIDAD & TOBAGO
Lake Nicaragua   Ríohacha   Coro   Port of Spain
COSTA RICA San José   Barranquilla   Maracaibo   Cumaná Güiria Trinidad   10° N
Chirripó 3819   Cartagena Valledupar   Barquisimeto Valencia Maracay Barcelona   Maturín Tigre
    Panama Canal Colón   Sincelejo   Lake Maracaibo Acarigua   Orinoco Delta
Panama City   Montería   Barinas   Ciudad Bolívar R. Orinoco   Ciudad Guayana   1
Isthmus of Panama David Aguadulce   Turbo   Cúcuta San Cristóbal   San Fernando de Apure   Embalse de Guri El Callao
PANAMA   COLOMBIA Bucaramanga   VENEZUELA   El Tigre
    Medellín   Sierra Nevada del Cocuy 5493   Llanos   R. Meta   Guiana Highlands
85° W   80° W   75° W   70° W   65° W   5° N

H   I   J   K   L

NORTH AMERICA

Caribbean Sea

ATLANTIC OCEAN

Key to symbols
- Countries
- ■ Capital city
- ○ Important city/town

Total population of South America
396 million

Barranquilla
Maracaibo
Caracas
Port of Spain
TRINIDAD AND TOBAGO

VENEZUELA
Georgetown
GUYANA
Paramaribo
SURINAME
Cayenne
FRENCH GUIANA

Medellín
Bogotá
COLOMBIA
Cali

Largest country
Brazil 8 514 879 sq km

Quito
ECUADOR
Belém
São Luís
Country with most people
Brazil 196 655 000

Galapagos Islands
(Ecuador)
Guayaquil
Iquitos
Manaus
Fortaleza

B R A Z I L
Natal

Trujillo
PERU
Recife

Lima
Aracaju
Salvador

PACIFIC OCEAN

Lake Titicaca
BOLIVIA
La Paz
Brasília
Belo Horizonte

Largest city
São Paulo 21 028 000

Arequipa
Sucre

Antofagasta
PARAGUAY
Asunción
São Paulo
Rio de Janeiro

C
H
I
L
E

A R G E N T I N A
Curitiba

Valparaíso
Santiago
Porto Alegre

ATLANTIC OCEAN

Concepción
Buenos Aires
URUGUAY
Montevideo

The British Isles at the same scale.

Juan Fernandez Islands
(Chile)

Mar del Plata

Other maps showing regions of South America are on pages: 48-49
48-49 South America

Punta Arenas
Tierra del Fuego

Falkland Islands
(UK)

South Georgia
(UK)

South Orkney Islands
(UK)

Antarctic Peninsula

The statue known as Christ the Redeemer over-looks Rio de Janeiro.

The ruins of the lost Inca city of Machu Picchu in Peru.

0   400   800   1200   1600   2000 km

Scale : One centimetre on this map is the same as 400 kilometres on the ground.

Key to symbols

Land height above sea level in metres

over 5000
2000 – 5000
1000 – 2000
500 – 1000
200 – 500
0 – 200

Aconcagua ▲ 6959 Mountain and height in metres

〜 River

Lake

Seasonal lake

N
W E
S

Total area of South America
17 815 420 sq km

Caribbean Sea

ATLANTIC OCEAN

Lake Maracaibo

Orinoco Delta

R. Orinoco

Angel Falls

Mount Roraima 2810

Llanos

Guiana Highlands

Mouths of the Amazon

Longest river
River Amazon 6516 km

R. Japurá

R. Negro

R. Amazon

Amazon Basin

Selvas

R. Amazon

R. Madeira

Galapagos Islands

R. Purus

Largest lake
Lake Titicaca 8340 sq km

Andes

Altiplano

Lake Titicaca

Atacama Desert

R. Tocantins

R. São Francisco

Brazilian Highlands

PACIFIC OCEAN

Highest mountain
Aconcagua 6959 m

Nevado Ojos del Salado ▲ 6908

Gran Chaco

R. Paraguay

R. Paraná

R. Salado

Aconcagua ▲ 6959

R. Paraná

R. Uruguay

Juan Fernandez Islands

ATLANTIC OCEAN

Pampas

Rio de la Plata

R. Colorado

R. Negro

Isla de Chiloé

Valdes Peninsula

Patagonia

Andes

Largest island
Tierra del Fuego 47 000 sq km

Falkland Islands

Tierra del Fuego

Cape Horn

South Georgia

Antarctic Peninsula

South Orkney Islands

400   800   1200   1600   2000 km

Wild horses in Patagonia, Argentina.

The Amazon rain forest covers more than one third of Brazil.

Scale : One centimetre on this map is the same as 400 kilometres on the ground.

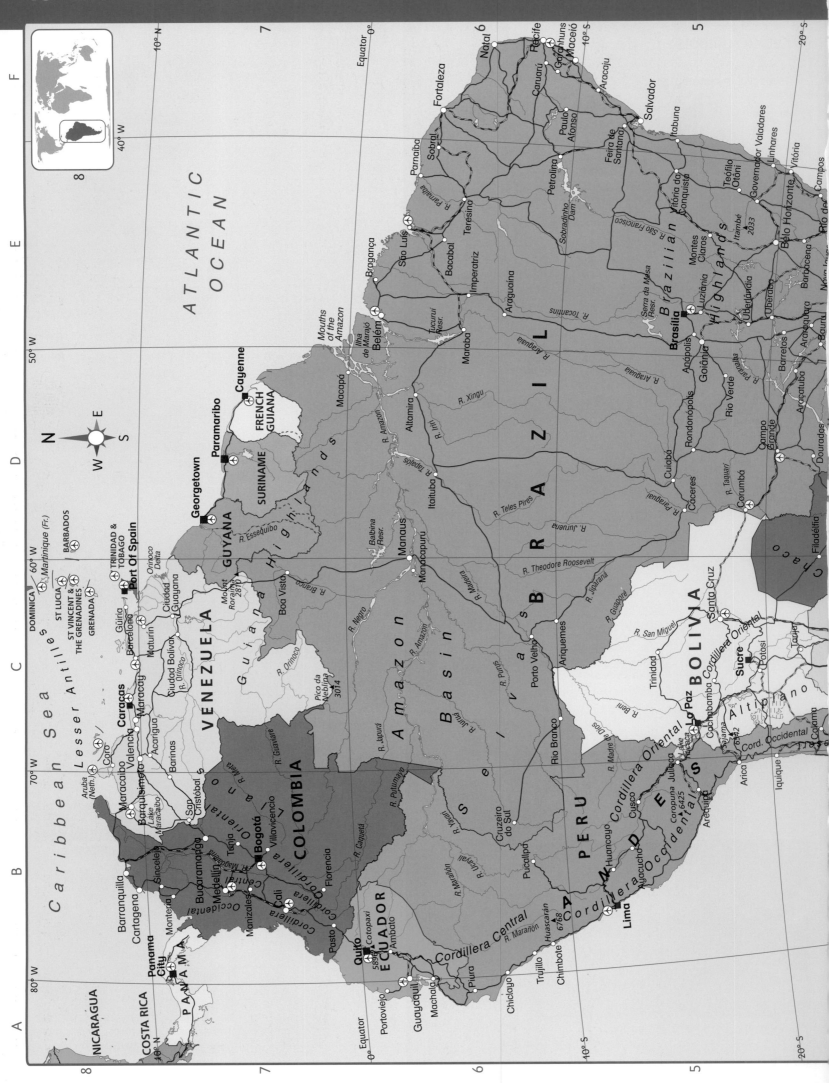

Scale : One centimetre on this map is the same as 200 kilometres on the ground.

0   200   400   600   800 km

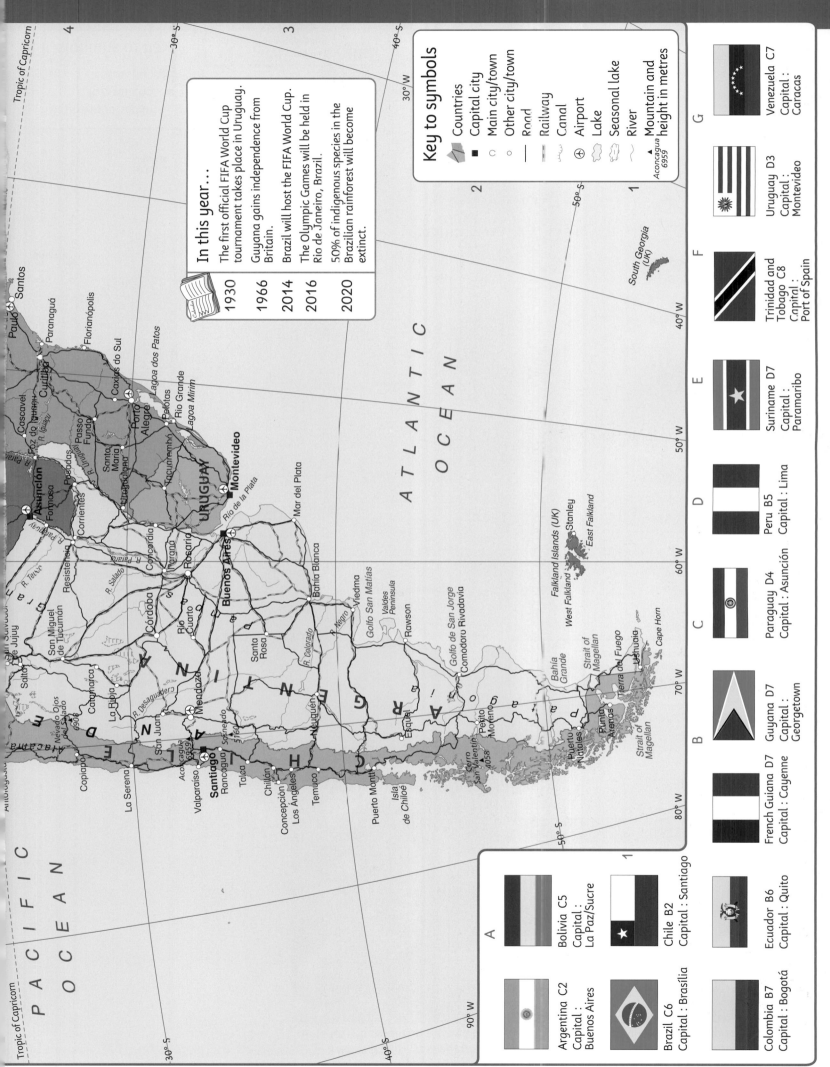

In this year...

1930	The first official FIFA World Cup tournament takes place in Uruguay.
1966	Guyana gains independence from Britain.
2014	Brazil will host the FIFA World Cup.
2016	The Olympic Games will be held in Rio de Janeiro, Brazil.
2020	50% of indigenous species in the Brazilian rainforest will become extinct.

Key to symbols

- Countries
- ■ Capital city
- ○ Main city/town
- ○ Other city/town
- Road
- Railway
- Canal
- ⊕ Airport
- Lake
- Seasonal lake
- River
- ▲ Mountain and height in metres
  Aconcagua 6959

A

Argentina C2
Capital : Buenos Aires

Brazil C6
Capital : Brasília

Colombia B7
Capital : Bogotá

Bolivia C5
Capital : La Paz/Sucre

Chile B2
Capital : Santiago

Ecuador B6
Capital : Quito

B

French Guiana D7
Capital : Cayenne

Guyana D7
Capital : Georgetown

C

Paraguay D4
Capital : Asunción

D

Peru B5
Capital : Lima

E

Suriname D7
Capital : Paramaribo

F

Trinidad and Tobago C8
Capital : Port of Spain

G

Uruguay D3
Capital : Montevideo

Venezuela C7
Capital : Caracas

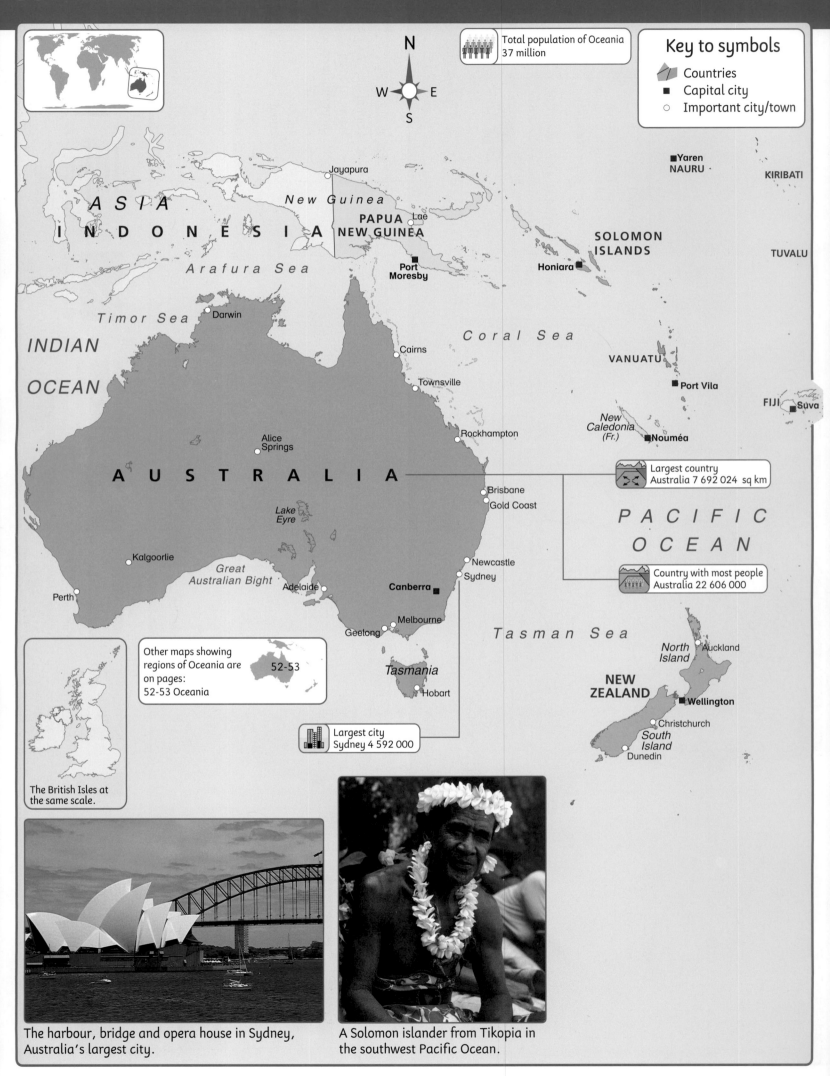

Total population of Oceania
37 million

Key to symbols

- Countries
- ■ Capital city
- ○ Important city/town

Yaren
NAURU

KIRIBATI

Jayapura

New Guinea

ASIA

INDONESIA

PAPUA
NEW GUINEA

Lae

TUVALU

SOLOMON
ISLANDS

Honiara

Arafura Sea

**Port
Moresby**

Timor Sea

Darwin

INDIAN

OCEAN

Coral Sea

Cairns

Townsville

VANUATU

Port Vila

New
Caledonia
(Fr.)

FIJI ■ **Suva**

Rockhampton

■ **Nouméa**

Alice
Springs

A U S T R A L I A

Largest country
Australia 7 692 024 sq km

P A C I F I C

O C E A N

Lake
Eyre

Brisbane
Gold Coast

Country with most people
Australia 22 606 000

Kalgoorlie

Great
Australian Bight

Newcastle
Sydney

Perth

Adelaide

Canberra ■

Melbourne

Geelong

Tasman Sea

North
Island

Auckland

Other maps showing
regions of Oceania are
on pages:
52-53 Oceania

52-53

Tasmania

NEW
ZEALAND

Hobart

Wellington

Christchurch

South
Island

Dunedin

The British Isles at
the same scale.

Largest city
Sydney 4 592 000

The harbour, bridge and opera house in Sydney,
Australia's largest city.

A Solomon islander from Tikopia in
the southwest Pacific Ocean.

0 300 600 900 1200 1500 km   Scale : One centimetre on this map is the same as 325 kilometres on the ground.

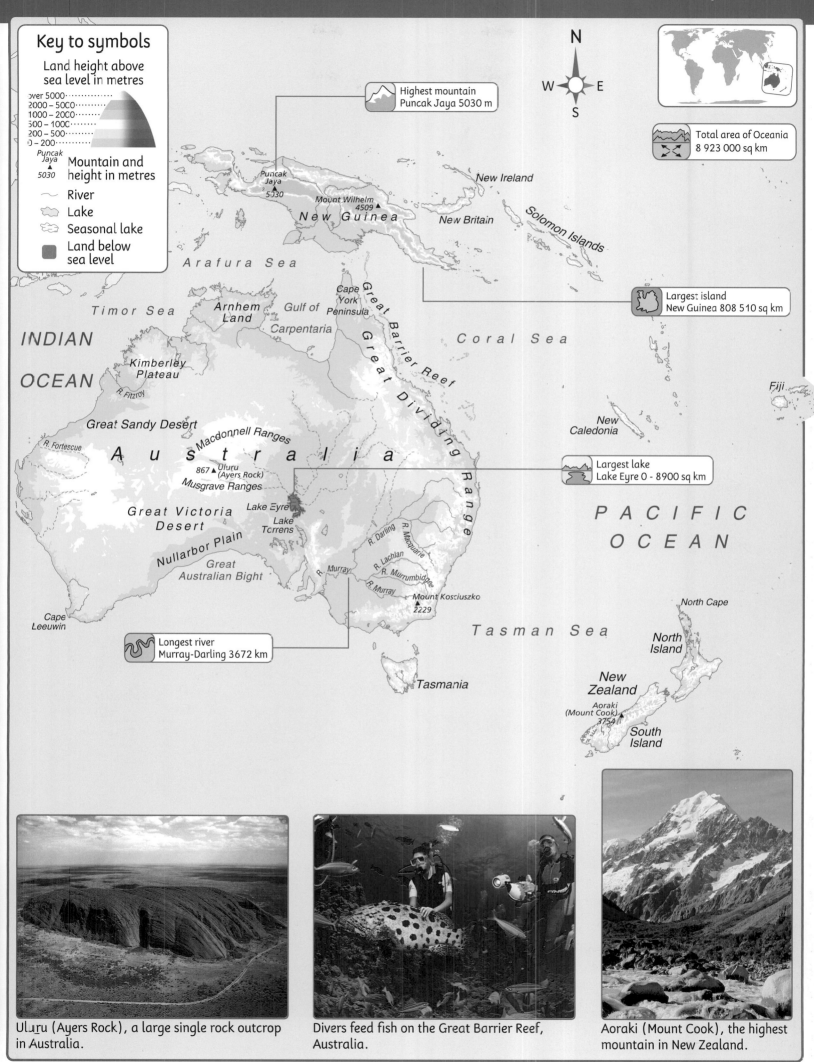

Key to symbols

Land height above sea level in metres

- over 5000
- 2000 – 5000
- 1000 – 2000
- 500 – 1000
- 200 – 500
- 0 – 200

Puncak Jaya ▲ 5030   Mountain and height in metres

⟋ River

Lake

Seasonal lake

Land below sea level

Highest mountain
Puncak Jaya 5030 m

Total area of Oceania
8 923 000 sq km

Largest island
New Guinea 808 510 sq km

Largest lake
Lake Eyre 0 - 8900 sq km

Longest river
Murray-Darling 3672 km

N
W   E
S

INDIAN OCEAN

Timor Sea

Arafura Sea

Arnhem Land

Gulf of Carpentaria

Cape York Peninsula

New Guinea

Puncak Jaya 5030

Mount Wilhelm 4509 ▲

New Ireland

New Britain

Solomon Islands

Coral Sea

Great Barrier Reef

Kimberley Plateau

R. Fitzroy

Great Sandy Desert

R. Fortescue

Macdonnell Ranges

A u s t r a l i a

867 ▲ Uluru (Ayers Rock)

Musgrave Ranges

Great Victoria Desert

Lake Eyre

Lake Torrens

Great Dividing Range

New Caledonia

Fiji

R. Darling

R. Macquarie

R. Lachlan

R. Murrumbidgee

R. Murray

Nullarbor Plain

Great Australian Bight

R. Murray

Mount Kosciuszko 2229

PACIFIC OCEAN

Cape Leeuwin

Tasman Sea

Tasmania

North Cape

North Island

New Zealand

Aoraki (Mount Cook) 3754

South Island

Uluru (Ayers Rock), a large single rock outcrop in Australia.

Divers feed fish on the Great Barrier Reef, Australia.

Aoraki (Mount Cook), the highest mountain in New Zealand.

0   300   600   900   1200   1500 km

Scale : One centimetre on this map is the same as 325 kilometres on the ground.

Key to symbols

Countries
Capital city
Main city/town
Other city/town
Road
Railway
Puncak Jaya 5030

Airport
Lake
Seasonal lake
River
Mountain and height in metres

Scale : One centimetre on this map is the same as 200 kilometres on the ground.

0 200 400 600 800 km

160° E 170° E 180° 170° W

N
W · E
S

NAURU

KINGSMILL GROUP

KIRIBATI

SOLOMON
ISLANDS

TUVALU

Phoenix
Islands

Choiseul
Santa Isabel
Malaita
Honiara
Guadalcanal
San Cristobal

Funafuti
Vaiaku

Tokelau
(New Zealand)

10° S

VANUATU

Espiritu Santo

Malakula

Éfaté
Port Vila

Wallis and
Futuna Islands
(France)

SAMOA

Savai'i
Upolu
Apia

American
Samoa
(USA)

5

Vanua Levu

FIJI

Viti Levu
Suva

New Caledonia
(France)

Îles
Loyauté

Nouméa

Niue
(New Zealand)

Nuku'alofa   TONGA

20° S

Tropic of Capricorn

P A C I F I C   O C E A N

4

30° S

North Cape

North Island
Auckland
Manukau
Hamilton

Calendar
In this year...

2007 Sydney Opera House is listed as a
World Heritage Site.

2009 Over 170 people die in the worst wild
fires in Australia's history.

2011 Two earthquakes 4 months apart hit
Christchurch, New Zealand and kill
over 180.

2011 Samoa and Tokelau move from east to
west of the International Date Line.

n Sea

NEW

Mount Taranaki
(Mount Egmont)
2518

ZEALAND

Palmerston
North

Napier

Nelson

Wellington

3

Aoraki
(Mount Cook)
3754
Southern Alps

South Island

Christchurch

Chatham Islands
(New Zealand)

40° S

Cape Providence

Lake
Te Anau

Dunedin

2

Auckland Islands
(New Zealand)

50° S 180° 170° W 160° W

F   G   H   I   J

Australia B4
Capital :
Canberra

6

Fiji G5
Capital : Suva

Kiribati H6
Capital : Bairiki

Nauru F6
Capital : Yaren

5

New Zealand G2
Capital :
Wellington

Papua New
Guinea D6
Capital :
Port Moresby

4

Samoa H5
Capital : Apia

Solomon
Islands F6
Capital : Honiara

3

Tonga H4
Capital :
Nuku'alofa

Tuvalu G6
Capital : Vaiaku

2

Vanuatu F5
Capital :
Port Vila

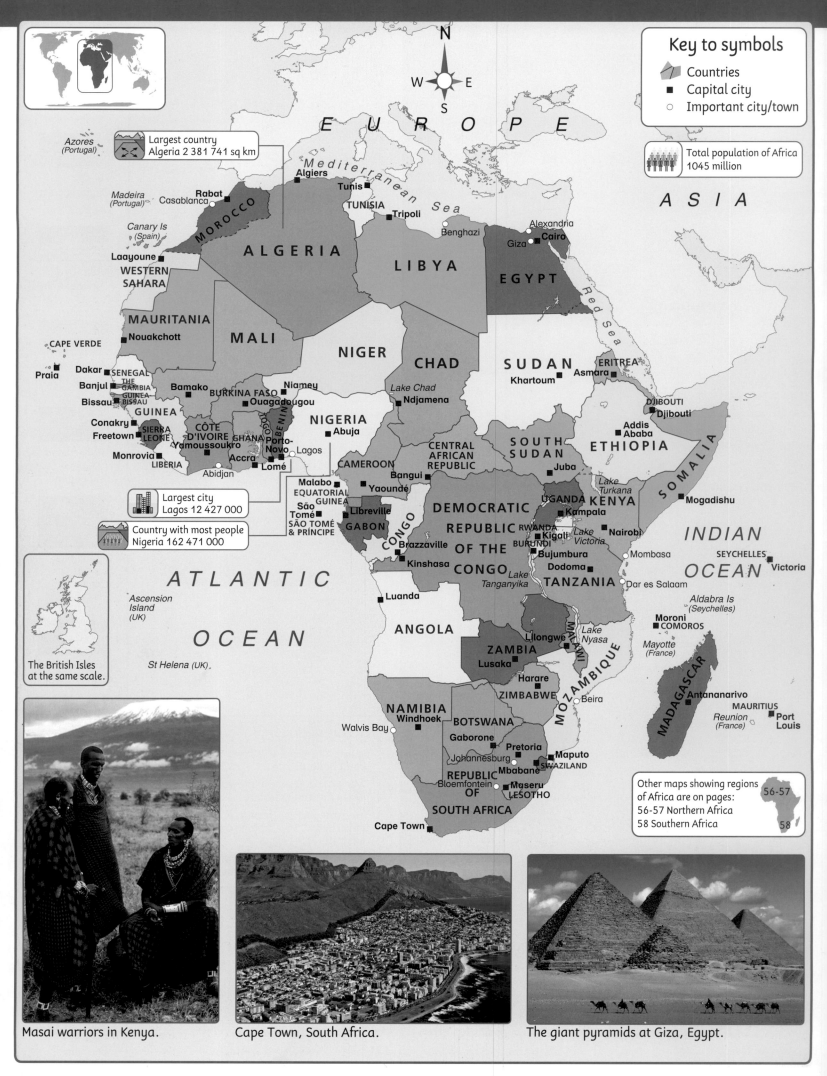

Key to symbols

- Countries
- ■ Capital city
- ○ Important city/town

Total population of Africa 1045 million

Largest country
Algeria 2 381 741 sq km

Largest city
Lagos 12 427 000

Country with most people
Nigeria 162 471 000

EUROPE

N
W E
S

ASIA

Mediterranean Sea

Azores (Portugal)

Madeira (Portugal)

Canary Is (Spain)

Algiers
Tunis
TUNISIA
Tripoli
Benghazi
Alexandria
Cairo
Giza

MOROCCO
Rabat
Casablanca
Laayoune
WESTERN SAHARA
ALGERIA
LIBYA
EGYPT
Red Sea

CAPE VERDE
Praia

MAURITANIA
Nouakchott
MALI
NIGER
CHAD
SUDAN
Khartoum
ERITREA
Asmara

Lake Chad
Ndjamena
DJIBOUTI
Djibouti

Dakar
SENEGAL
THE GAMBIA
Banjul
GUINEA BISSAU
Bissau
Bamako
BURKINA FASO
Ouagadougou
Niamey

GUINEA
Conakry
Freetown
SIERRA LEONE
CÔTE D'IVOIRE
Yamoussoukro
GHANA
TOGO
BENIN
Porto-Novo
Accra
Lomé
Abidjan
Monrovia
LIBERIA
NIGERIA
Abuja
Lagos

CENTRAL AFRICAN REPUBLIC
Bangui
SOUTH SUDAN
Juba
ETHIOPIA
Addis Ababa
SOMALIA
Mogadishu

CAMEROON
Yaoundé
Malabo
EQUATORIAL GUINEA
São Tomé
SÃO TOMÉ & PRÍNCIPE
GABON
Libreville
CONGO
DEMOCRATIC REPUBLIC OF THE CONGO
Brazzaville
Kinshasa

UGANDA
Kampala
KENYA
Nairobi
Lake Turkana
RWANDA
Kigali
BURUNDI
Bujumbura
Lake Victoria
Mombasa
TANZANIA
Dodoma
Dar es Salaam
Lake Tanganyika

INDIAN OCEAN
SEYCHELLES
Victoria

Aldabra Is (Seychelles)

ATLANTIC OCEAN

Ascension Island (UK)

St Helena (UK)

Luanda
ANGOLA

ZAMBIA
Lusaka
MALAWI
Lilongwe
Lake Nyasa
Mayotte (France)
Moroni
COMOROS

MADAGASCAR
Antananarivo
MAURITIUS
Reunion (France)
Port Louis

NAMIBIA
Windhoek
Walvis Bay
BOTSWANA
Gaborone
ZIMBABWE
Harare
Beira
MOZAMBIQUE

Johannesburg
Pretoria
Maputo
SWAZILAND
Mbabane
REPUBLIC OF SOUTH AFRICA
Bloemfontein
Maseru
LESOTHO
Cape Town

The British Isles at the same scale.

Other maps showing regions of Africa are on pages:
56-57 Northern Africa
58 Southern Africa

56-57
58

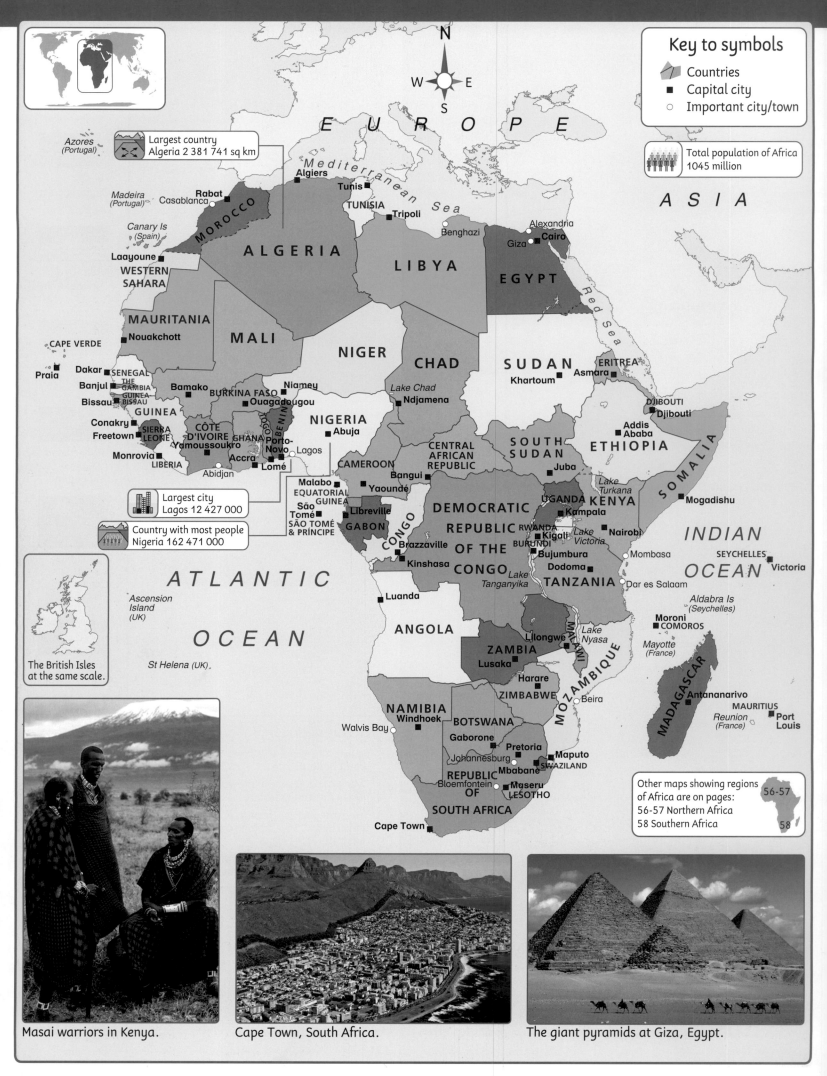
Masai warriors in Kenya.

Cape Town, South Africa.

The giant pyramids at Giza, Egypt.

0 450 900 1350 1800 2250 km

Scale : One centimetre on this map is the same as 450 kilometres on the ground.

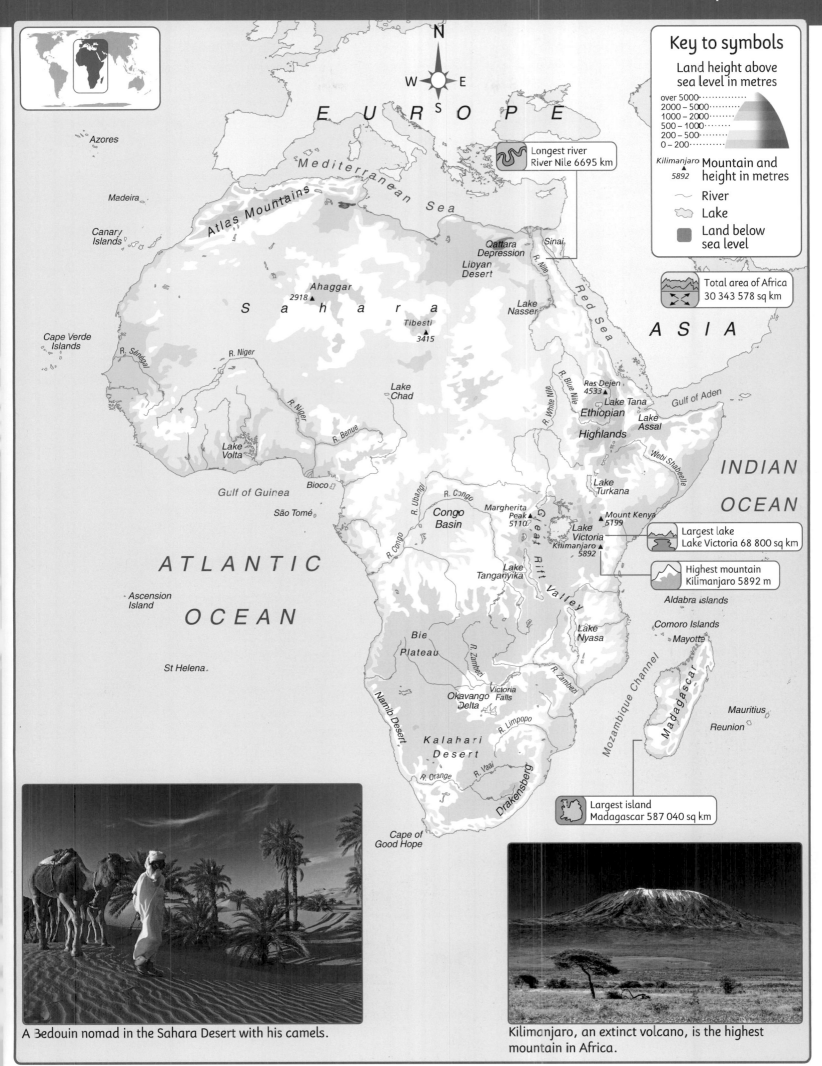

Key to symbols

Land height above sea level in metres

over 5000
2000 – 5000
1000 – 2000
500 – 1000
200 – 500
0 – 200

Kilimanjaro ▲ 5892 — Mountain and height in metres

River

Lake

Land below sea level

Total area of Africa 30 343 578 sq km

Longest river River Nile 6695 km

Largest lake Lake Victoria 68 800 sq km

Highest mountain Kilimanjaro 5892 m

Largest island Madagascar 587 040 sq km

N W S E

EUROPE

ASIA

Mediterranean Sea

Azores

Madeira

Canary Islands

Cape Verde Islands

Atlas Mountains

Qattara Depression

Sinai

Libyan Desert

Ahaggar 2918 ▲

Sahara

Tibesti 3415 ▲

Lake Nasser

R. Nile

Red Sea

Gulf of Aden

R. Sénégal

R. Niger

R. Niger

R. Benue

Lake Chad

Lake Volta

Gulf of Guinea

Bioco

São Tomé

R. Blue Nile

Ras Dejen 4533 ▲

Lake Tana

Ethiopian Highlands

Lake Assal

R. White Nile

Webi Shabeelle

Lake Turkana

INDIAN OCEAN

R. Ubangi

R. Congo

Congo Basin

Margherita Peak ▲ 5110

R. Congo

Mount Kenya ▲ 5199

Lake Victoria

Kilimanjaro ▲ 5892

Great Rift Valley

Lake Tanganyika

ATLANTIC OCEAN

Ascension Island

St Helena

Bie Plateau

Lake Nyasa

Aldabra Islands

Comoro Islands

Mayotte

Namib Desert

R. Zambezi

Okavango Delta

Victoria Falls

R. Zambezi

Madagascar

Mozambique Channel

Mauritius

Reunion

Kalahari Desert

R. Limpopo

R. Orange

R. Vaal

Drakensberg

Cape of Good Hope

A Bedouin nomad in the Sahara Desert with his camels.

Kilimanjaro, an extinct volcano, is the highest mountain in Africa.

0   450   900   1350   1800   2250 km

Scale : One centimetre on this map is the same as 450 kilometres on the ground.

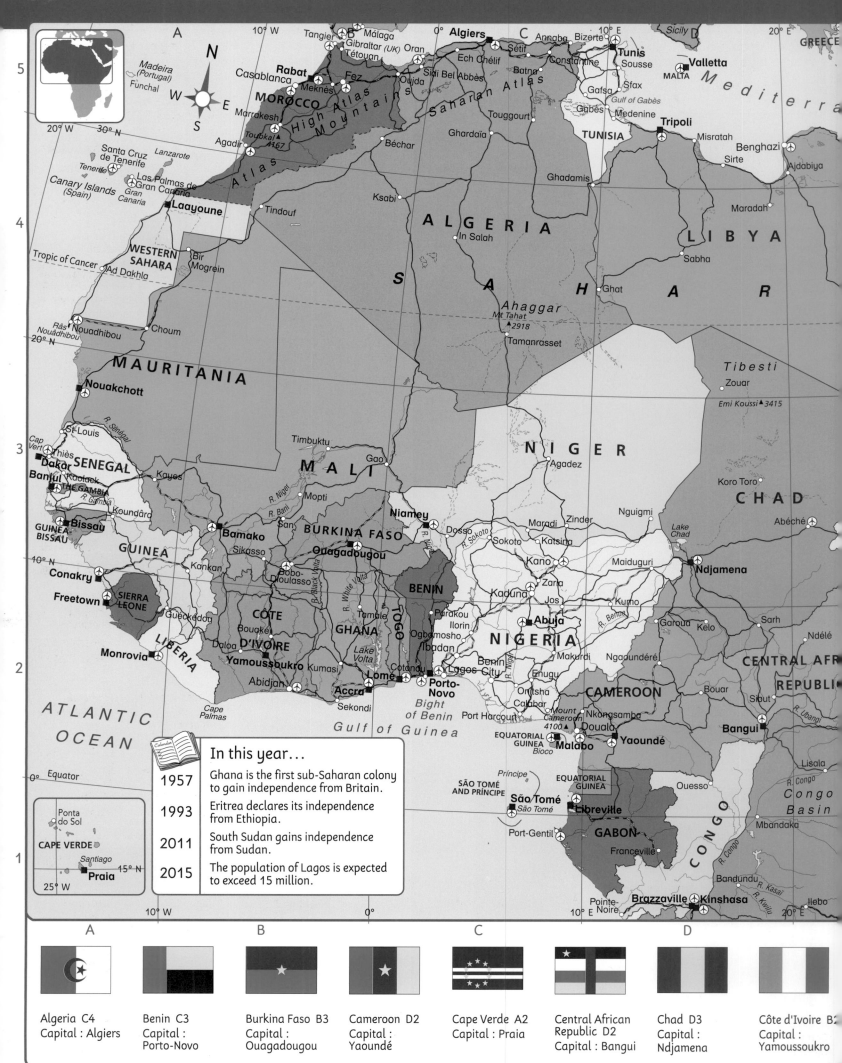

In this year...

1957	Ghana is the first sub-Saharan colony to gain independence from Britain.
1993	Eritrea declares its independence from Ethiopia.
2011	South Sudan gains independence from Sudan.
2015	The population of Lagos is expected to exceed 15 million.

Algeria C4
Capital : Algiers

Benin C3
Capital : Porto-Novo

Burkina Faso B3
Capital : Ouagadougou

Cameroon D2
Capital : Yaoundé

Cape Verde A2
Capital : Praia

Central African Republic D2
Capital : Bangui

Chad D3
Capital : Ndjamena

Côte d'Ivoire B2
Capital : Yamoussoukro

0   200   400   600   800 km

Scale : One centimetre on this map is the same as 200 kilometres on the ground.

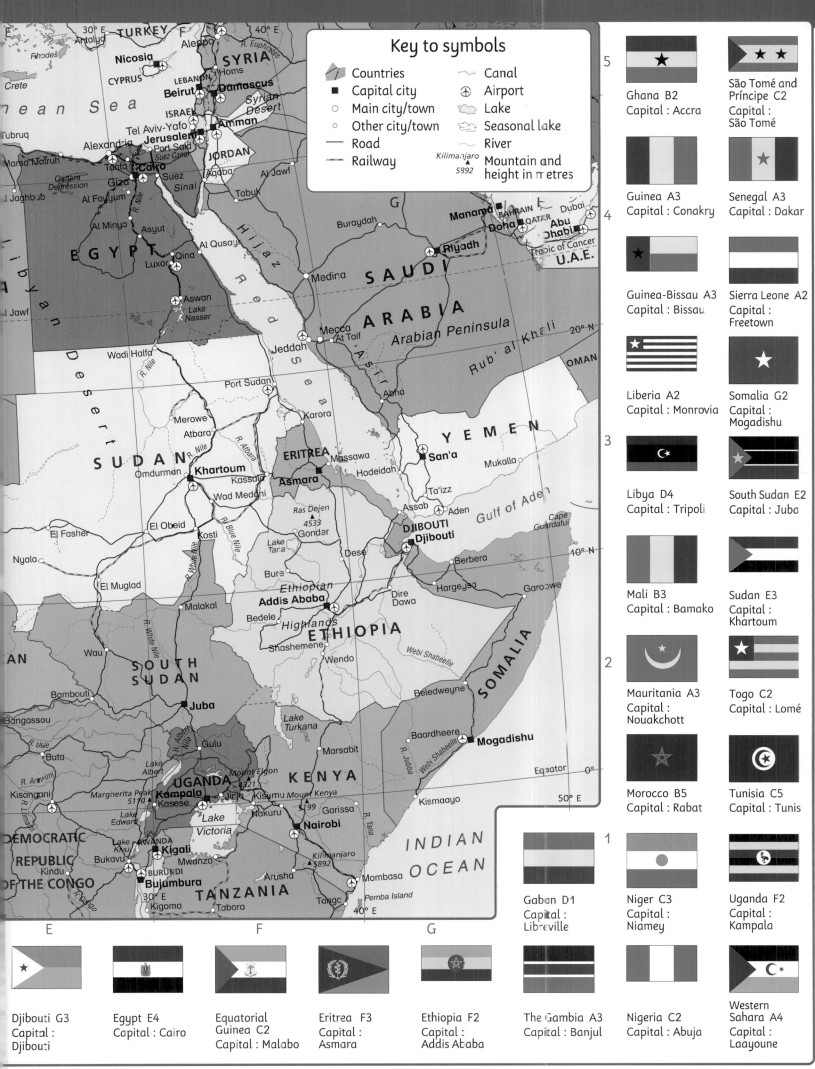

Key to symbols

- Countries
- ■ Capital city
- ○ Main city/town
- ○ Other city/town
- — Road
- Railway
- Canal
- Airport
- Lake
- Seasonal lake
- River
- Kilimanjaro 5892 Mountain and height in metres

Ghana B2 Capital : Accra

São Tomé and Príncipe C2 Capital : São Tomé

Guinea A3 Capital : Conakry

Senegal A3 Capital : Dakar

Guinea-Bissau A3 Capital : Bissau

Sierra Leone A2 Capital : Freetown

Liberia A2 Capital : Monrovia

Somalia G2 Capital : Mogadishu

Libya D4 Capital : Tripoli

South Sudan E2 Capital : Juba

Mali B3 Capital : Bamako

Sudan E3 Capital : Khartoum

Mauritania A3 Capital : Nouakchott

Togo C2 Capital : Lomé

Morocco B5 Capital : Rabat

Tunisia C5 Capital : Tunis

Gabon D1 Capital : Libreville

Niger C3 Capital : Niamey

Uganda F2 Capital : Kampala

Djibouti G3 Capital : Djibouti

Egypt E4 Capital : Cairo

Equatorial Guinea C2 Capital : Malabo

Eritrea F3 Capital : Asmara

Ethiopia F2 Capital : Addis Ababa

The Gambia A3 Capital : Banjul

Nigeria C2 Capital : Abuja

Western Sahara A4 Capital : Laayoune

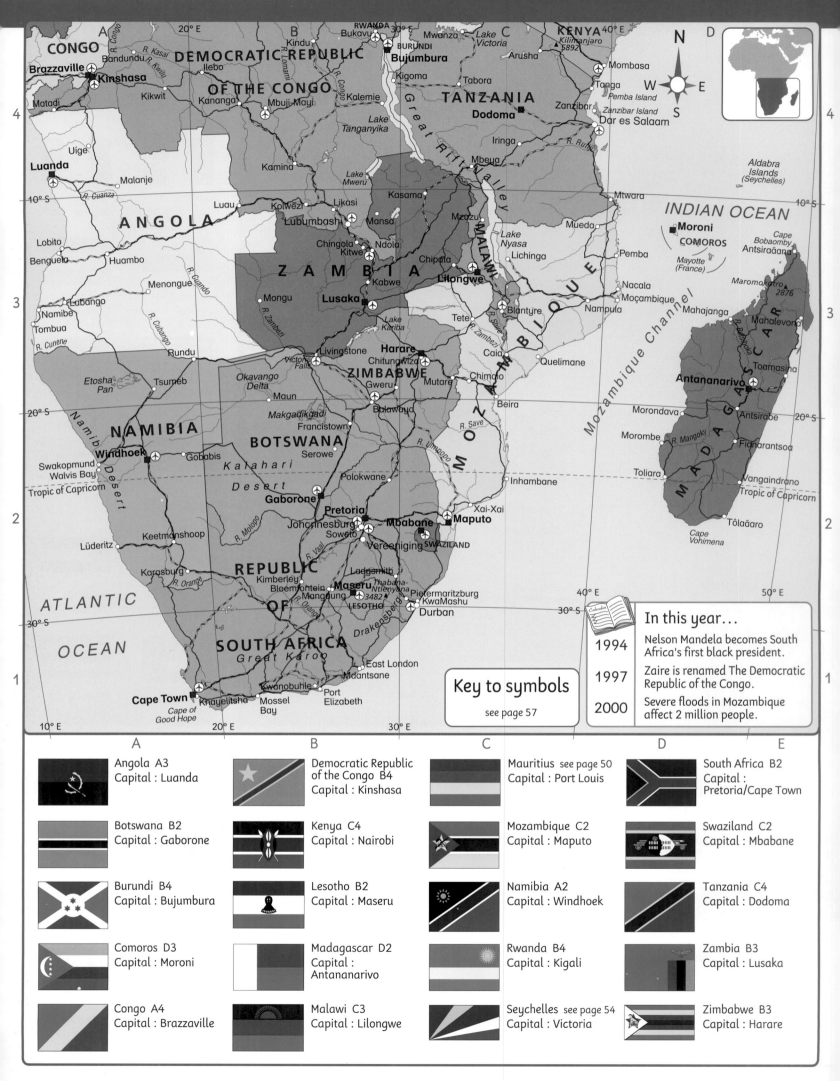

A   20° E   B   RWANDA   30° E   C   KENYA   40° E   D

CONGO
Brazzaville
Kinshasa
Matadi
Bandundu R. Kwilu R. Kasai
Ilebo
Kikwit
Kananga
Mbuji-Mayi
DEMOCRATIC REPUBLIC
OF THE CONGO
R. Congo
R. Lomami
Kindu
Bukavu
BURUNDI
Bujumbura
Kigoma
Tabora
Mwanza
Lake Victoria
Arusha
Kilimanjaro
5892
Mombasa
Tanga
Pemba Island

Uíge
Luanda
Lobito
Benguela
Malanje
R. Cuanza
10° S
Lubango
Namibe
Tombua
R. Cunene
ANGOLA
Luau
Luena
Kamina
Kolwezi Likasi
Lubumbashi
Chingola Kitwe
Ndola
Lake Mweru
Kasama
Mzuzu
Mansa
Lake Tanganyika
Kalemie
TANZANIA
Dodoma
Zanzibar
Zanzibar Island
Dar es Salaam
Iringa
Mbeya
R. Ruhu
Mtwara
Aldabra Islands (Seychelles)

N
W   E
S

INDIAN OCEAN
Moroni
COMOROS
Mayotte (France)
Cape Bobaomby
Antsiraãana

Menongue
R. Cuando
R. Cubango
Rundu
ZAMBIA
Mongu
R. Zambezi
Kabwe
Lusaka
Lichinga
Lake Nyasa
MALAWI
Lilongwe
Chipata
Tete
R. Shire
Blantyre
Nacala
Moçambique
Nampula
Pemba
Maromokotro 2876
Mahajanga
Mahalevona
MADAGASCAR
R. Betsiboka

20° S
Etosha Pan
Tsumeb
NAMIBIA
Namib Desert
Windhoek
Swakopmund
Walvis Bay
Tropic of Capricorn
Okavango Delta
Maun
Livingstone
Victoria Falls
Makgadikgadi
Francistown
Gobabis
Kalahari
Desert
Serowe
BOTSWANA
Harare
Chitungwiza
Gweru
ZIMBABWE
Bulawayo
Mutare
R. Zambezi
Caia
Chimoio
Beira
R. Save
Quelimane
MOZAMBIQUE
R. Limpopo
Inhambane
Morondava
Morombe
R. Mangoky
Toliara
Mozambique Channel
Antananarivo
Antsirabe
Fianarantsoa
Vangaindrano
Tropic of Capricorn
Tôlaãaro
Cape Vohimena

Lüderitz
Keetmanshoop
Karasburg
R. Molopo
Gaborone
Johannesburg
Pretoria
Soweto
Vereeniging
Mbabane
SWAZILAND
Maputo
Xai-Xai

REPUBLIC
OF
SOUTH AFRICA
R. Orange
Kimberley
Bloemfontein
Mangaung
Ladysmith
Maseru
LESOTHO
Thabana-Ntlenyana 3482
Pietermaritzburg
KwaMashu
Durban
Drakensberg

30° S
ATLANTIC
OCEAN
R. Orange
R. Vaal
Great Karoo
East London
Mdantsane
Cape Town
Khayelitsha
Kwanobuhle
Mossel Bay
Port Elizabeth
Cape of Good Hope

40° E   50° E

Key to symbols
see page 57

In this year...
1994 Nelson Mandela becomes South Africa's first black president.
1997 Zaire is renamed The Democratic Republic of the Congo.
2000 Severe floods in Mozambique affect 2 million people.

A   B   C   D   E

Angola A3
Capital : Luanda

Democratic Republic of the Congo B4
Capital : Kinshasa

Mauritius see page 50
Capital : Port Louis

South Africa B2
Capital : Pretoria/Cape Town

Botswana B2
Capital : Gaborone

Kenya C4
Capital : Nairobi

Mozambique C2
Capital : Maputo

Swaziland C2
Capital : Mbabane

Burundi B4
Capital : Bujumbura

Lesotho B2
Capital : Maseru

Namibia A2
Capital : Windhoek

Tanzania C4
Capital : Dodoma

Comoros D3
Capital : Moroni

Madagascar D2
Capital : Antananarivo

Rwanda B4
Capital : Kigali

Zambia B3
Capital : Lusaka

Congo A4
Capital : Brazzaville

Malawi C3
Capital : Lilongwe

Seychelles see page 54
Capital : Victoria

Zimbabwe B3
Capital : Harare

0   200   400   600   800 km

Scale : One centimetre on this map is the same as 200 kilometres on the ground.

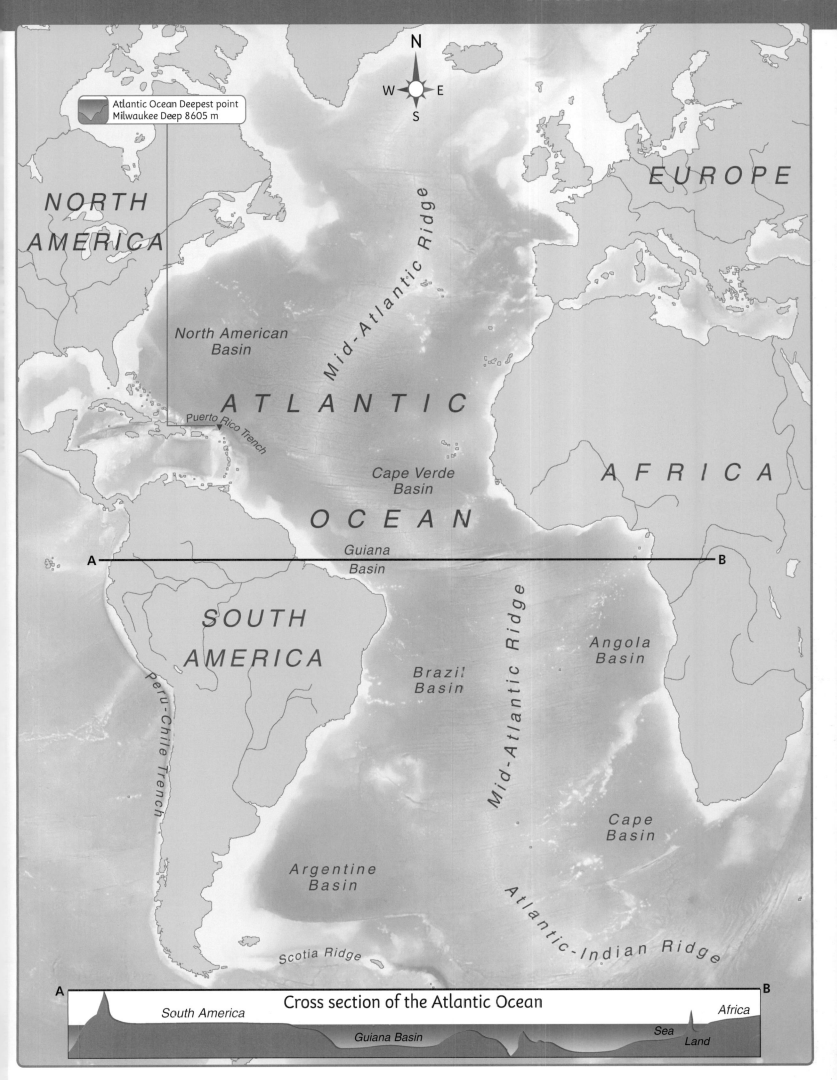

NORTH
AMERICA

Atlantic Ocean Deepest point
Milwaukee Deep 8605 m

N
W E
S

EUROPE

North American
Basin

Mid-Atlantic Ridge

A T L A N T I C

Puerto Rico Trench

AFRICA

Cape Verde
Basin

O C E A N

Guiana
Basin

A   B

SOUTH
AMERICA

Mid-Atlantic Ridge

Angola
Basin

Brazil
Basin

Peru-Chile Trench

Cape
Basin

Argentine
Basin

Atlantic-Indian Ridge

Scotia Ridge

A   Cross section of the Atlantic Ocean   B

South America

Africa

Guiana Basin

Sea

Land

Indian Ocean

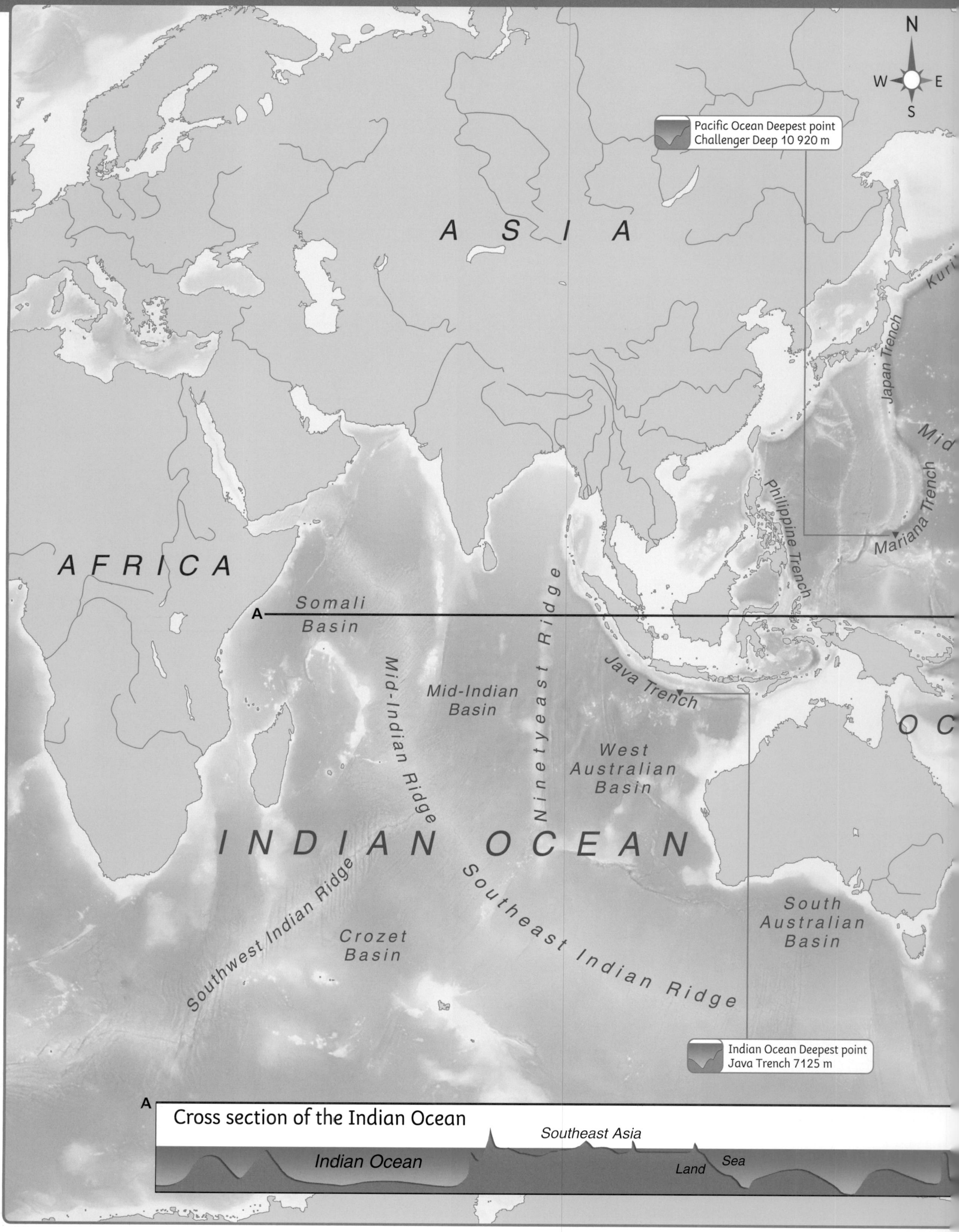
N
W
E
S
Pacific Ocean Deepest point
Challenger Deep 10 920 m
A S I A
Kuril
Japan Trench
Mid
Mariana Trench
Philippine Trench
A F R I C A
A
Somali
Basin
Mid-Indian Ridge
Mid-Indian
Basin
Ninetyeast Ridge
Java Trench
West
Australian
Basin
OC
I N D I A N   O C E A N
Southwest Indian Ridge
Crozet
Basin
Southeast Indian Ridge
South
Australian
Basin
Indian Ocean Deepest point
Java Trench 7125 m
A
Cross section of the Indian Ocean
Southeast Asia
Indian Ocean
Land
Sea

Trench

Aleutian Trench

Northwest
Pacific
Basin

NORTH
AMERICA

Northeast
Pacific
Basin

Hawaiian Ridge

Pacific Mountains

Central
Pacific
Basin

PACIFIC

Middle America Trench

East Pacific Rise

B

SOUTH
AMERICA

OCEAN

EANIA

Norfolk Island Ridge

Kermadec Trench

Tonga Trench

Southwest
Pacific
Basin

Peru
Basin

Pacific-Antarctic Ridge

Peru-Chile Trench

Southeast
Pacific
Basin

Cross section of the Pacific Ocean

B

South America

Pacific Ocean

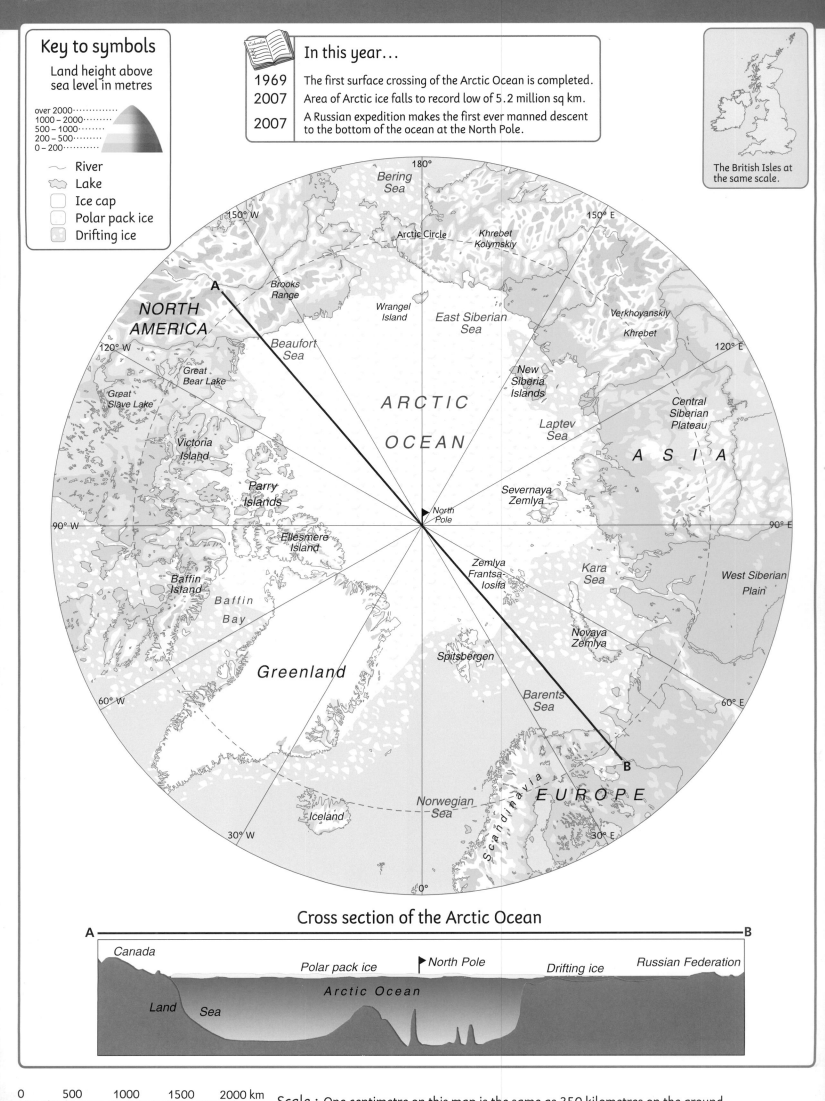

Key to symbols

Land height above sea level in metres

over 2000 ··············
1000 – 2000 ············
500 – 1000 ··········
200 – 500 ··········
0 – 200 ··········

∿ River
Lake
Ice cap
Polar pack ice
Drifting ice

In this year...

1969   The first surface crossing of the Arctic Ocean is completed.
2007   Area of Arctic ice falls to record low of 5.2 million sq km.
2007   A Russian expedition makes the first ever manned descent to the bottom of the ocean at the North Pole.

The British Isles at the same scale.

180°

Bering Sea

150° W

Arctic Circle

Khrebet Kolymskiy

150° E

Brooks Range

NORTH AMERICA

Wrangel Island

East Siberian Sea

Verkhoyanskiy Khrebet

120° W

Beaufort Sea

120° E

Great Bear Lake

Great Slave Lake

New Siberia Islands

Central Siberian Plateau

A S I A

Victoria Island

Laptev Sea

Parry Islands

Severnaya Zemlya

90° W

North Pole

90° E

Ellesmere Island

A R C T I C   O C E A N

Zemlya Frantsa-Iosifa

Kara Sea

West Siberian Plain

Baffin Island

Baffin Bay

Novaya Zemlya

Greenland

Spitsbergen

60° W

Barents Sea

60° E

Scandinavia

Norwegian Sea

E U R O P E

Iceland

30° W

30° E

0°

Cross section of the Arctic Ocean

A ——— B

Canada

Polar pack ice   ▶ North Pole   Drifting ice   Russian Federation

Land   Sea

Arctic Ocean

0   500   1000   1500   2000 km

Scale : One centimetre on this map is the same as 350 kilometres on the ground.

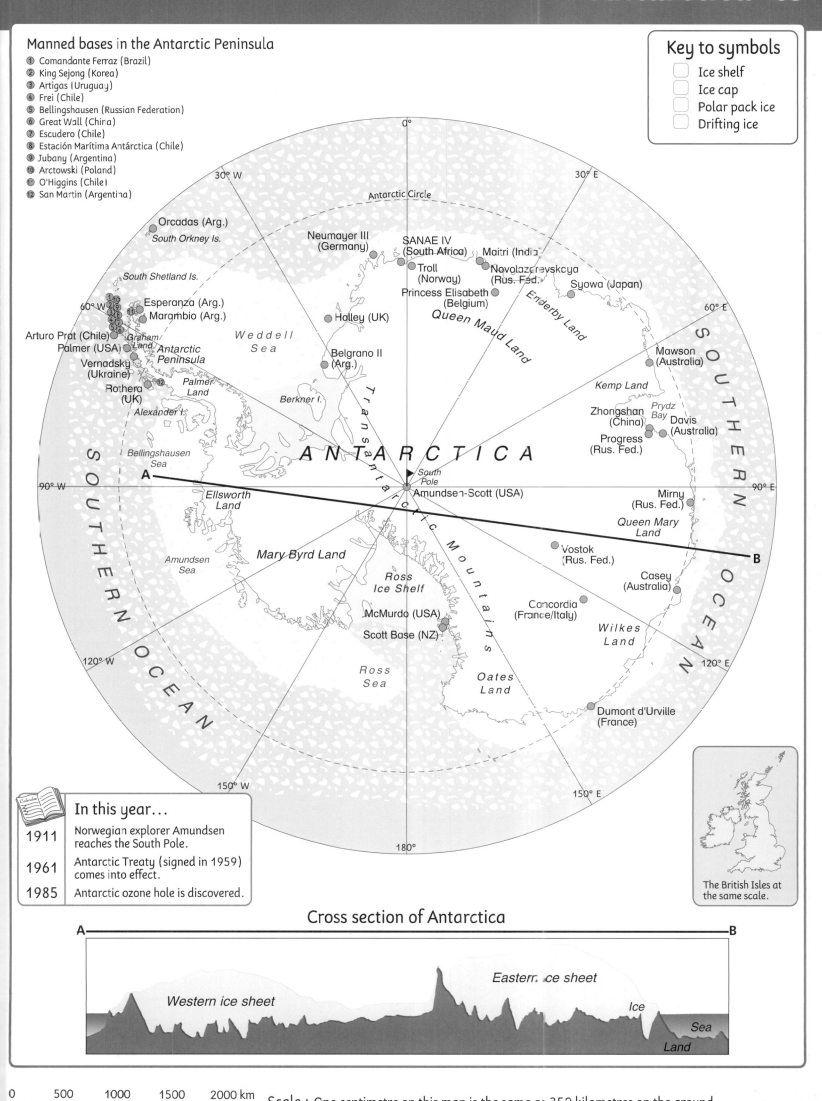

Manned bases in the Antarctic Peninsula

① Comandante Ferraz (Brazil)
② King Sejong (Korea)
③ Artigas (Uruguay)
④ Frei (Chile)
⑤ Bellingshausen (Russian Federation)
⑥ Great Wall (China)
⑦ Escudero (Chile)
⑧ Estación Marítima Antárctica (Chile)
⑨ Jubany (Argentina)
⑩ Arctowski (Poland)
⑪ O'Higgins (Chile)
⑫ San Martin (Argentina)

Key to symbols

Ice shelf
Ice cap
Polar pack ice
Drifting ice

In this year...

1911	Norwegian explorer Amundsen reaches the South Pole.
1961	Antarctic Treaty (signed in 1959) comes into effect.
1985	Antarctic ozone hole is discovered.

The British Isles at the same scale.

Cross section of Antarctica

Western ice sheet

Eastern ice sheet

Ice

Sea

Land

0   500   1000   1500   2000 km

Scale : One centimetre on this map is the same as 350 kilometres on the ground.

place name	grid code	place name	grid code	place name	grid code	place name	grid code
Cairo *capital* 57 F5		Tyne *river* 22 D4		Italy *country* 28 G3		Corsica *island* 28 F3	
page number		page number		page number		page number	
cities and towns are shown in green		water features are shown in blue		countries and states are shown in red		physical features are shown in black	

Photo credits
Science Photo Library:
p19 London, p20 UK Satellite image, p21 Beachy Head

Lick Observatory:
p10 Moon

NASA:
p10 Earth, p11 globe, Reto Stockli

Mark Steward:
p21 Glen Coe, p30 Kuala Lumpur, p39 Grand Canyon, p50 Sydney

Corbis:
p38 Times Square, Jose Fuste Raga, p46 Rio de Janeiro, Richard T. Nowitz

Shutterstock:
p8 Sun, p8 Solar System, pp8-9 Mercury, Venus, Earth, Mars, Sun, Jupiter, Saturn, Uranus, and Neptune, all Antony McAulay, p11 Sun, xfox01, p16 Colosseum, SF photo, p16 Eiffel Tower, Igor Rivilis, p17 Norway, Plotnikoff, p31 Rice paddies, Bali, Lim Yong Hian, p31 Mount Everest, Pichugin Dmitry, p38 Washington, Jonathan Larsen, p39 Niagara Falls, Howard Sandler, p46 Machu Picchu, Amy Nicole Harris, p51 Aoraki (Mount Cook), Sander van Sinttruye, p54 Cape Town, W. Woyke, p54 Giza, sculpies, p55 Kilimanjaro, enote

Robert Harding Picture Library:
p17 Etna eruption, Otto Hahn, p18 Brussels, Wim Van Cappellen, p30 Shanghai, Markus Dlouhy, p47 Argentina, Galen Rowell, p47 Rainforest, Jacques Jangoux, p50 Solomon islander, K. Hympendahl, p51 Great Barrier Reef, Fred Bavendam, p51 Uluru, Raimund Franken, p54 Masai warriors, Friedrich Stark, p55 Sahara Desert, Frans Lemmens

Acknowledgement
Editorial Adviser: Professor Simon Catling, pp2-7

Maps on the pages listed below are derived in part from material originally published in Collins Longman Atlases:
Keystart Junior Atlas: pp12-13, p16, pp26-27, pp28-29, p30, p38, p46, p50, p54. Foundation Atlas: p62, p63